# The Planting of the Churches in South Africa

# The Planting of the Churches in South Africa

*by*

JANE M. SALES

WILLIAM B. EERDMANS PUBLISHING COMPANY
GRAND RAPIDS, MICHIGAN

# EDITORIAL FOREWORD

There is no area of the world where Americans in general are more bewildered about the composition and distribution of the churches, their interrelationships, and their attitudes towards social issues, race relations, and governmental policies than South Africa. Literature on the planting and growth of the churches there has scarcely been available. In this book Mrs. Jane M. Sales attempts to fill that gap. She shows how the course of mission expansion in South Africa was affected by the constant antagonism between the Boer and British elements among the white settlers, by the white man's hunger for the land, and by the absence of a system of comity such as usually characterized missions in other parts of the world. Mission action by Englishmen, Scots, Germans, Americans, Frenchmen, Scandinavians, Swiss, and native-born Reformed churchmen of the region have raised up churches of whites, blacks, coloured, Indians — some of these churches comprehensive and inclusive, but many of them separated and segregated — distinguished by tribe, language, or imported denominational traditions. In reaction to factors and forces evident in this record, South African Christians have appropriated the Christian faith in their own cultural terms and have created what the white man calls "separatist churches." Having read this book, one understands why the problems of Christian unity are even more complex and difficult to resolve in South Africa than in other countries.

This book is one of the historical surveys of the series "Discipling the Nations" in *Christian World Mission Books,* which is a comprehensive collection of paperback volumes on every aspect of the world mission of the church of Christ. Authors are recruited from among many nations and churches. These are books for teachers and students, for pastors and laymen, for the general public. Sound scholarship underlies them, but scholarly apparatus is kept at the minimum. A large place will be given to Africa, because Africa will soon have the largest Christian community in all the world.

R. Pierce Beaver
*Editor*

5

# CONTENTS

# PREFACE

This is a short book and many of the most fascinating details about the church in South Africa have had to be left out. Many societies whose efforts have contributed to the missionary history of South Africa have been mentioned only briefly, or not at all, because of lack of space. The early part of the story has been told in greater detail than the later. One might argue that too much space has been given to the London Missionary Society. In defense, I could say that since it was first in the field in many areas, it met many of the problems first, the same problems which other societies met. I must admit, however, that my Congregationalist sympathies may have influenced me.

A few words about terminology:

1) Tribal names are often prefixed with "Ba" because in most Bantu languages the "ba" prefix means the plural of the personal class of nouns; "u" or "mu" is usually the singular.

2) The term "landdrost" is used occasionally. The English equivalent is magistrate, the local representative of the national government.

3) Denominational names. I have used the term Methodist throughout, even though the more common term in the nineteenth century was Wesleyan. I have used Presbyterian for the missionaries of the Glasgow Missionary Society, and for both groups of Scottish missionaries even after the Disruption of 1843.

I am indebted to many: to my neighbors at the Federal Theological Seminary, especially Dr. Donald Cragg for his helpful comments and Mrs. Gillian Hawkes for her typing; to the staff of the Killie Campbell Library in Durban; and to my children, Mark, Anne, and Jimmy, for putting up with a lot. Most of all, I thank Dick, my husband, who encouraged me to tackle this book in the first place, who made the maps for it, and who helped me in innumerable ways to get it finished.

Jane M. Sales

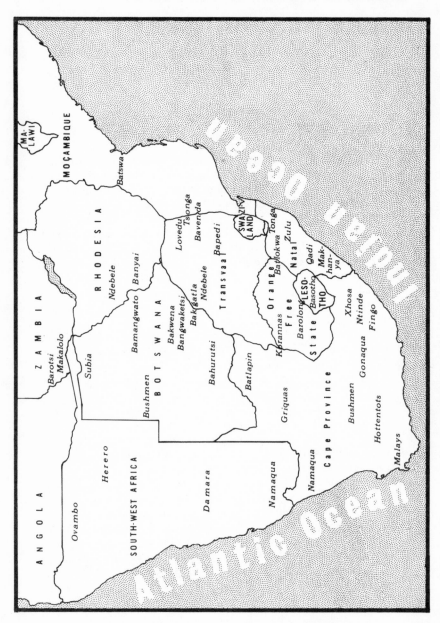

**Original Tribal Homes of Tribes Mentioned in the Text**

# I

# THE CHURCH IN THE DUTCH COLONY

The Republic of South Africa is an independent nation of approximately 18 million people at the southern end of the continent of Africa. Of these 18 million people, more than two-thirds are descendants of the Bantu (African) peoples who during the last thousand years have moved southwards through the eastern part of the continent from the highlands of Ethiopia and the lake region. Where they came from before that is largely a matter of conjecture. About one-sixth (3 million) of the people of South Africa are white, or "European" in the common usage of South Africa, the descendants of the Dutch, German, and French immigrants of the seventeenth and eighteenth centuries, the British immigrants of the nineteenth century, and a smattering of people from everywhere who have come in the twentieth century. The remainder are classified in South Africa as "Coloured" and "Asiatic." The Coloured people trace their ancestry to a variety of sources: Hottentot, Bushman, European, Malayan, and African. The Asiatic people are largely Indian, primarily located in Natal; their forefathers came to South Africa either as farm laborers to work on the sugar plantations or as traders. The white population generally considers itself divided in the proportion of about sixty to forty, Afrikaans-speaking over English-speaking. With the exception of the Jewish community, which is everywhere present but strong only in the Johannesburg area, all whites in South Africa consider themselves "Christian." Of the African (Bantu) population, probably

11

about two-thirds consider themselves Christian. More or less all of the Coloured group are Christian (except for the Malays who are Muslim), but not more than about 5 percent of the Indians are Christians. Of the non-Christian Indians, about four-fifths are Hindu, the remainder Muslim.

Christian churches are, obviously, an important part of the social scene in South Africa. In an African community the church and the school are likely to be the only community buildings — and in many the school and church are one, with the church meeting in the school building. In an Afrikaans farming community the Dutch Reformed church is at least as important, the place where thoughts are molded for all areas of life. In the urban areas, where English-speaking people are more common, the role of the churches is not so decisive; for most people here, business and sports associations are probably more influential than the churches.

From the time of the Portuguese exploration until the end of the nineteenth century when the Suez Canal was opened, South Africa, especially Cape Town, was one of the real crossroads of the world. Though the Portuguese were the first Europeans (at least in modern times) to circumnavigate Africa, they made little use of the few natural harbors. The reason for this was that they soon controlled Angola and the coast of Mozambique, both of which were far more profitable as trading posts. On one of the very early trips around the Cape, the Portuguese built a chapel at Mossel Bay with the expectation that ships might get water there, but the same expedition on its return trip discovered St. Helena Island, which was more convenient for the purpose. Most of the Portuguese experiences on the coast of South Africa were connected with shipwrecks, leaving a trail of legends of shipwrecked sailors becoming incorporated into the African population of Natal and the Transkei. This may be the background of some very light-skinned Zulu and Xhosa people, but these events left no heritage of European culture or Christian teaching.

In 1630 a Portuguese ship, the *Sao Goncalo,* was wrecked at Plettenberg Bay. Those who survived stayed there for eight months, planting and harvesting crops, and trading with the local inhabitants, who were presumably Hottentots. They built a church there. More than half the crew had died in the wreck, but more than a hundred survived, including five friars. Some of these eventually made their way to India, again leaving no permanent imprint on South Africa.

They did, however, leave an interesting account of the Hottentot people whom they came to know. They reported:

> These savages are not quite black, they go about naked, with a small piece of skin round their loins, in winter they add to this capes of the same, they wear copper bracelets on their arms, and round their necks the sinews of oxen. They make their bodies stink by anointing them with the excrement of oxen. . . . No sign of religious worship. . . .

English ships regularly stopped at the Cape during the first half of the seventeenth century. An English chaplain wrote of the Hottentots: "... the sun shines not upon a people in the whole world more barbarous . . . beasts in the skins of men, rather than men in the skins of beasts; as may appear by their ignorance, habit, language, diet; with other things, which makes them most brutish."[1] The fact that a Hottentot who had been taken to England reverted to "barbarism" on his return was taken as proof that these people were too degraded to be uplifted. Another English visitor of about the same time wrote of the Hottentots: "... no place of worship, no day of rest, no order in Nature, no shame, no truth, no ceremony in births, or burials, meer brutishness and stupidness wholly shadowing them."[2]

Considering these descriptions of the Hottentots, it is quite surprising to read the report of two of the crew of the *Haarlem,* a Dutch ship wrecked in Table Bay (Cape Town). These two survivors of the *Haarlem,* after their five months' stay at Table Bay, wrote a *Remonstrance* to the directors of the Dutch East India Company (the Council of Seventeen) about the desirability of the Cape as a revictualling station on the way to India. The *Remonstrance* claimed that the Hottentots were friendly and willing to trade. It asserted that the unfortunate experiences some had had at the Cape with people being killed by the "natives" were due to the Hottentots' feeling that the Europeans had stolen their sheep and cows. The Dutch East India Company was urged to take the Cape as a business proposition and also as an opportunity to spread the true Reformed Christian Religion. The Hottentots were considered by these men to be quite teachable and it was expected that they could be trained as servants of the Company.

But the man who was appointed in 1652 as commander of the expedition to establish such a refreshment station at Table Bay took a somewhat different view of the natives. Writing just four years after the wreck of the *Haarlem*, Jan Van Riebeeck said about the

*Remonstrance:* "Though 'Sieur' Leendert does not seem to have any fear of the natives, I beg to state as my opinion that they are not to be trusted, being a brutal gang, living without any conscience." He added, however, "the statement that the natives or their children are able to learn the Dutch language is important and a very good thing, but of greater moment is the furtherance of our Reformed Christian Religion about which he appears to be sanguine."[3]

Yet, in spite of the expressed desire of the Company to extend the Reformed Christian Religion, no ordained minister was appointed at the Cape of Good Hope during the first thirteen years. The purpose of this "cabbage patch on the way to India" was expressed by de Kiewiet:

> The Dutch East India Company had no desire to tame the wilderness, nor to find new homes for Dutchmen over the sea. Jan Van Riebeeck's duty would be done if he provided the Company's vessels with fresh meat and vegetables, for the settlement at the Cape was not a separate venture. It was a cog in a great commercial system which every year yielded those dividends which were the envy of English merchants and the despair of Colbert and his French trading companies. In that system spices and profits came before souls and patriotism. The golden book of St. Francis Xavier and the obscure martyrs who died of African fevers are all but empty pages in the annals of Dutch colonial effort.[4]

The fact that Holland was at this time, in the middle of the seventeenth century, the epitome of culture in Europe did not greatly affect developments at the Cape, because the Company had no intention of creating a colony there. They expected to send only enough men to grow the vegetables they wanted and a small garrison to man a fort there. They expected to obtain meat by bartering with the Hottentots for the sheep and cattle they possessed. The fact that the Cape became a colony was due, not to Company policy, but to circumstance.

Jan Van Riebeeck, his wife, his daughter, his two nieces, and his staff of Company servants arrived at the Cape on April 6, 1652. The religious services of the community were to be provided for the community by the "sick-visitor," Willem Wylant. Wylant had brought his wife with him, and they were the first to move out of tents into the partially completed wooden fort in June of 1652, in time for the birth of Wylant's son, the first white child born at the

Cape. Wylant's job was to lead in daily prayers and to read the sermon on Sunday. Since he was not an ordained minister, he did not have the right to preach his own sermons, or to baptize, or to administer the Lord's Supper. The sacraments were available only when a ship with a clergyman aboard stopped at the Cape. The sick-visitor was responsible for whatever education took place, but during the first few years Wylant was more often sent off on trading expeditions to the Hottentots than engaged in any educational effort. He did attempt to teach some of the Hottentot youth to read and write, but the discipline required for such an effort was impossible for the boys. There were few, if any, children of school age among the Dutch for the first several years, since most of the men of the garrison were unmarried or had left their wives in Holland. Presumably because of his duties to the sick, Wylant and his family lived in the same building which housed the sick. The groom and the horses also lived there. The various apartments were divided by walls made of reeds. In 1655 Wylant was injured by a leopard, and the next year he was invalided to Batavia.

The first few months of life at the Cape were especially hard; many died of dysentery, food was scarce, and the tents were inadequate in the violent storms and cold weather. On the 12th May, 1652, the Lord's Supper was celebrated at the Cape for the first time. At this entry in his journal Van Riebeeck wrote:

> In the still uncovered part of the house inside the square of the unfinished fort, everybody standing, the Reverend Backerius, a minister who came with the *Walvis,* held the first sermon, and the Lord's Supper was celebrated. May the merciful blessing of the Almighty rest on the work still to be done. Amen.[5]

Attendance at public worship was required of all the men at the Cape during Van Riebeeck's time. The first time one failed to attend, a week's wine ration was withheld. For repeated offences, the punishment was public work in chains for a year. The men were even fined for failing to say grace at meals. The smallness of the community and closeness of its communal life continued for the first five years. But the creation of a group of "free burghers" in 1657 and the introduction of slaves in 1658 changed this pattern of life.

During the early years at the Cape, relations with the Hottentots were of crucial importance. The instructions of the Company to Van Riebeeck were that the Hottentots must be treated with the utmost kindness in order to keep the peace and to encourage them to trade their stock to the Dutch for meat to supply the passing ships. Though Van Riebeeck himself considered them a "brutal gang," his orders were that "Nobody may hit, shove, or in any manner ill-use the Hottentots." The murder of a Dutch herdboy by a group of Hottentots who sought to take back some animals they had sold to the Company made relations very difficult for a time. But this was a rare incident — very few Dutch lost their lives to the Hottentots, though stock-thefts have been a South African problem ever since. Van Riebeeck considered several schemes to avoid this problem by separating the Hottentots from the Dutch community. One he proposed was a typically Dutch idea — to build a canal across the Cape Peninsula; another which was actually carried out a little later was to plant a hedge. The hedge was planted, but the Dutch themselves refused to be bound by it.

Van Riebeeck received recurring reports about tribes to the north who had immense herds of cattle. Emissaries were sent, and sometimes they succeeded in buying enough cattle for the needs of ships, but more often Van Riebeeck was plagued by the need to acquire more meat. Within a very short time the Hottentots in the neighbourhood of the Cape were without sufficient stock for their own needs.

Though a number of Hottentots became economically involved in the Dutch community, and many of them addicted to the "firewater," with which they were often paid for their animals, none of the men are recorded as having been baptized or as having sought baptism. At least three Hottentot women, however, were baptized. The best known of these was Eva, who had worked in Van Riebeeck's household and often acted as his interpreter. In the year that he left the Cape, 1662, Eva was publicly baptized. Later she was married by Christian rites to a Dane who was employed by the Company as surgeon's assistant. By baptism Eva had acquired the privileges and rights enjoyed by any white woman at the Cape at that time. In her later years, however, she was confined to Robben Island, where she could maintain only a very modest life. The other two Hottentot women were Sara and Cornelia, contemporaries of Eva who became Europeanized.

Sara committed suicide in 1671 by hanging herself after she had been deceived by a European who had promised to marry her. . . . Cornelia appears to have been the least unfortunate of the three, for she lived to a ripe old age, having discarded her European ways and returned to her skins and her own people.[6]

The shortage of women in the Dutch community might have driven more men to take Hottentot wives, but the arrival of slaves provided a more attractive alternative. Almost from the beginning of the settlement, Van Riebeeck had begged the Company to send him slaves to do the gardening and such work, because the soldiers were not good workers. The first slaves which the Company agreed to let Van Riebeeck have were from a captured Portuguese slave ship. These arrived at the Cape in early 1658. The journal of Van Riebeeck for April 17, 1658 records:

> Fine morning. Arrangements were started for establishing a school for the Company's male and female slaves brought here by the *Amersfoort,* which had taken them off a prize Portuguese slaver. To encourage the slaves to attend and to hear or learn the Christian prayers, it is ordered that after school everyone is to receive a small glass of brandy and two inches of tobacco.[7]

The question of whether slave children should be baptized or not came up at the Cape. Van Arckel, the first ordained minister to be assigned to the Cape (he died six months after his arrival), baptized a number in 1665. But the very next year the debate which had raged in the East about whether slave children should be baptized or not (many felt that indiscriminate baptizing brought disgrace on the faith) flared up at the Cape when a passing minister baptized a white child but refused a slave child who was brought forward. Most of the congregation felt this as an affront both to it and to its minister, who had arranged for the baptisms. The Council of Policy, the local governing body made up of the Commander (later Governor) and senior officials, decided the following day that the usual practice of baptizing slave children would continue, and the next Sunday the refused child was baptized.

The baptism of adult slaves was not so eagerly sought, however, because baptism also conferred manumission. In the early days when most of the slaves were the property of the Company, this happened fairly often, but as the percentage of slaves owned by burghers increased, the climate of opinion turned definitely against the baptism of slaves. For the remainder of the seventeenth century, many slave babies continued to be baptized, because about three quarters of all babies born to slave mothers had white fathers and Company orders were that these must be baptized and manumitted when they reached a certain age. But as early as 1685 the Commissioner Van Rheede argued that the action of slave owners in forbidding their slaves to be baptized was withholding from them the joys of future life as well as their freedom in this life. This argument does not seem to have convinced many. In the eighteenth century, in an effort to enable more slaves to be baptized, the law requiring manumission of baptized slaves was changed to one requiring only that baptized slaves not be sold by their master; even this, however, was considered by the owners to be a transgression of the rights of private property and the owners saw to it that their slaves were not baptized. Slave owners often encouraged their slaves to accept Islam, so that the slaves had some of the benefits of religion without any pecuniary loss to their owners.

The advent of slavery at the Cape, coming as it did at the same time as the beginning of the free burghers, meant that from the first, the burgher society, which had been envisioned as a peasant society, was in fact a slave-owning society. Most of the free burghers came from the ranks of the Company's soldiers. Such were not always of the highest society — many were "impressed" into service, others were handed over to the Company by their families, who considered them black sheep. Honest, hardworking peasant types were rare. It is little wonder, then, that for many the great attractions of becoming free burghers were the opportunity to engage in illicit trade with the Hottentots and the chance to hunt in the wilds of Africa. For some, with plenty of slave labor to help them, wine production became a profitable undertaking. But it did not take more than one generation before the descendants of the tidy gardeners of Holland had become the wide-ranging, freedom-seeking frontiersmen of South Africa, following their cattle and sheep farther and farther into the interior.

Cape Town was, from the first, a settlement geared to the needs of passing ships. For visiting sailors and soldiers one of the major attractions in Cape Town was the slave lodge, where they queued up every evening to sleep with the female slaves. The model of upper-class life was that of the Company's officials at Batavia, but Cape Town did not come near any such opulence until late in the eighteenth century. Until then Cape Town was known to the world as a town in which practically every house doubled as a tavern for visiting seamen, and in which there was a large black-market.

In 1674 the first Church Council was organized. The Company paid all ministers, assigned them, and removed them from their posts. The ordinary form of Dutch Reformed Church government was established at Cape Town, but at all meetings of the Church Council the Company was represented by a political commissioner. All correspondence with the Church organization in the Netherlands was censored by the Company. The Church Council consisted of elders and deacons; the elders were elected by the congregation, the deacons nominated by the Church Council itself, but both had to be approved by the Council of Policy (the Governor and senior Company officials). In 1685 the church at Stellenbosch was organized with a Church Council and a minister. Stellenbosch was the first of the "interior" communities, where the needs and interests of the free burghers predominated over those of the Company. During the seventeenth century the ministers tried to open public church worship to all, but many of the white parishioners objected to sitting next to slaves and Hottentots because they considered them dirty and socially inferior. In their own homes, however, the burghers invited all the household, including the slaves, to evening family prayers. The head of the household read a portion from the Bible and prayed extemporaneously, and the whole household sang a psalm. This family ritual contributed greatly to the necessity of at least a modicum of reading ability among the farmers at the Cape, even among those who moved far beyond the bounds of church parishes.

During the time of Simon Van der Stel the most significant development at the Cape was the arrival of the French Huguenot refugees. The Company sent these people out to strengthen the burgher population in order to make the community agriculturally and militarily self-supporting. Until that time the Company had had to import rice from the East to feed the population of Cape Town; but by the beginning of the eighteenth century there were surpluses of foodstuffs at the Cape, which it was uneconomic to export. The skill of the French viniculturists enabled at least a portion of the Cape wine and brandy to be drinkable, which it had not been up to that time. The Company sent a French pastor with the French settlers in 1688, and French services were held alternately with Dutch services at Stellenbosch and Drakenstein (Paarl) until about 1725. The children of the refugees, however, were required to learn Dutch at school. Through intermarriage between the French and the

Dutch the two communities were merged by about 1750. The early years, however, had not always been harmonious; the French at Paarl had had to worship in a barn from 1689 to 1720, a matter the French considered to be discrimination against them. Their desire for separate French congregations had also been a bone of contention. But their common antagonism to the Company and its policies brought the French and Dutch burghers together. It is generally considered that the piety of the French was an important factor in the continued devotion of the burghers to their church during a period when its leadership was very weak and its main characteristic dry intellectualism.

The Dutch Reformed Church had a complete monopoly at the Cape during the period of the Company's rule. There were, however, occasionally visitors representing other churches. In 1685 and in 1687 French fleets with Jesuit priests aboard stopped for some time in Table Bay; they were on their way to and from Siam, where Louis XIV had sent them to learn about the Orient and to preach the gospel. Van der Stel permitted them to stay in a guest house in his garden (the building had originally been a tool shed, but had been enlarged to care for foreign dignitaries whom Van der Stel did not like to have staying in his own house). Roman Catholics among the colonists visited the priests and received their religious ministrations, during the first visit. But on the return visit the priests were not permitted to say mass. Whether this was due to the Revocation of the Edict of Nantes or Père Tachard's indiscretions in the book he published, or both, is uncertain.

Though there may have been many Roman Catholics at the Cape, it was not judicious for them to let their religious sympathies be known. There were, however, from the early years, many acknowledged Lutherans. And in 1742 they made their first appeal to have a resident pastor of their own. Until then, chaplains on Danish ships were permitted to hold Lutheran services only in private homes. The appeal was rejected, but was repeated from time to time. And finally, in 1780, the Lutherans received permission to build a church, although it was not permitted to have a steeple until many years later. This was the only non-Dutch Reformed church in the colony. Chaplains on English ships were permitted to conduct Anglican funerals in the Groote Kerk (the main church in Cape Town), when eminent people died at sea.

The eighteenth century was the period of Africanization in Dutch life at the Cape. Some immigrants did come, but the large families of the burgher farmers provided many more people. The vast expanses of available land to the north and east, though much of it not especially attractive, enabled the many sons of a farmer each to have a farm of his own. Whereas in 1700 the extent of the settled area was within a radius of fifty miles of Cape Town, by 1750 the radius was at least two hundred miles from Cape Town; by 1795 the extent was more than two hundred miles north and more than four hundred miles east. In the vicinity of Cape Town and Stellenbosch, farms were held in freehold and the population became fairly stable, with farms being passed down through the families. But on the frontier where the farms were held on loan from the Company, the farm buildings had to be auctioned: this meant that often none of the sons kept the place, usually moving on farther east or north. In rural areas during the eighteenth century, people lived in small houses with little furniture. For the men, hunting was the favorite pastime. The women lived a generally sedentary life, spent largely in needlework, leaving the heavy work to the domestic servants, either slave or Hottentot. The housewife presided over the distribution of the food, but after that spent her day sitting, sewing, and drinking coffee from the urn that was always hot beside her chair in the sitting-room. The whole family started the day at dawn with coffee and morning devotions, then work before breakfast. Evening devotions followed the evening meal.

The only book many families owned was a Bible; if a family owned any other books they were probably books of religious songs and sermons. These books were used in the family worship, which for most families was the only worship they had except for the quarterly *nagmaal* (Holy Communion). Those farthest from the parish centers could get to church only once a year, at Easter time. These quarterly and annual occasions were the social highlights of the farmers' lives. A few wealthy farmers had small houses near the parish church in Stellenbosch or Paarl (Drakenstein) for use on these occasions; most, however, stayed in their wagons, cooking out of doors. Church, family, and community were thus very much one.

Theal describes worship in the eighteenth-century Dutch churches in this way:

> The service commenced by the clerk giving out a psalm, and while this was being sung the clergyman in black gown and white bands entered the pulpit. Then followed the reading of

the ten commandments, the creed, and portions of the Bible. This was followed by another psalm. Before the sermon — which usually occupied an hour and a half or two hours in delivery — there was an *ex tempore* prayer, and after it a similar thanksgiving, during which the men stood but the women remained seated. The service closed with the singing of a psalm and the benediction. All was thus orderly; but these services in the grandeur of simplicity, though faultlessly correct in the opinion of the worshippers, were frequently so cold that they created little enthusiasm. Young people especially could not follow the minute subdivisions of a long sermon that had hardly any bearing upon their conduct in life.[8]

Whether hymns or only psalms should be sung in church was a matter of debate among the people. The opposition to hymns came from "a considerable section of the people, who feared innovation of any kind and desired to adhere to the psalms only as inspired by God."[9] Organs were in use in some of the churches. The psalms or hymns were sung by the whole congregation seated; there were no choirs.

In Cape Town great emphasis was laid on social position, as decreed by the Company. Seating in church was based on social precedence, and even the order in which the communicants received the sacrament followed this pattern. Men and women sat apart, but the women were arranged in order of rank according to their husbands' positions. In the rural areas, on the other hand, there was a great feeling of equality among all whites. Of course, many of them were cousins, if not brothers. There was no need for such benevolent organizations as orphanages, because children were an economic asset and there was always a well-to-do family to adopt homeless white children. When natural disasters struck, the community, widespread as it was, rallied round to provide shelter and a new start for the afflicted. Schools were almost totally lacking. In the few villages that existed, the minister or sick-visitor taught the elements of reading and writing.

In 1745 an effort was made to provide some kind of church organization beyond the parish level. The four clergymen in the colony, two elders from Cape Town, one elder from each of the other parishes, and Mr. Ryk Tulbagh, the Secunde (deputy governor), met under Mr. Tulbagh's leadership. At this time they laid out the boundaries of the parishes and decided to hold such a meeting annually. These meetings continued until 1759, but there were power struggles with both the Classis of Amsterdam and the Company. In 1759 the Company forbad any further meetings. By 1795, there were six parishes: Cape Town, Stellenbosch, Paarl, Tulbagh, Malmesbury, and Graaff-Reinet.

At the very end of the Company's dominion a new atmosphere began to make itself felt in the churches of the Cape. The evangelical revival was first expressed at the Cape in the preaching and teaching of the Reverend H. R. Van Lier. He was much concerned about conversion — both of the unevangelized heathen and of the burghers of the colony. His preaching was highly emotional. "Women were often moved to tears and sometimes fell into hysterics." Some of the men appreciated this sort of preaching, but others were very critical. Van Lier spent much time in home visitation, showing pastoral concern for his flock. He also worked hard to raise funds for a missionary effort in the lands of the Dutch East India Company, an enterprise which was to include a special theological training college in Holland for missionaries. The project eventually failed because of the economic problems of the Company,[10] and Van Lier died at the early age of twenty-eight, leaving behind a number of incomplete projects. But in 1794, a year after his death, another evangelical pastor came to the Cape. He was the Rev. Michael Christiaan Vos, who served as pastor at Roodezand (Tulbagh). He was particularly concerned for the evangelization of the slaves; he worked at this himself and persuaded many of his congregation to join in such efforts. These men were, however, rare in the eighteenth century. "By the end of the eighteenth century 'white man' and 'Christian' were synonymous terms; slave owners had ceased to favour conversion amongst the slaves; and farmers were objecting to the efforts by missionaries to convert and educate the Hottentots."[11]

By the end of the rule of the Company the people whom the Dutch had met first on their arrival, the Hottentots, had disappeared as a separate people, at least in the area within two hundred miles of Cape Town. The loss of their land to the Dutch farmers, of most of their cattle through trade with the whites, and of many of their lives through the smallpox epidemics that came from the East on the Company ships — because of these calamities, the Hottentots became a detribalized, landless proletariat. Those who kept the nearest semblance to their former way of life moved north along the

Atlantic coast into the dry areas of Namaqualand. These people called themselves Bastaards, later Griquas. The rest faced the choice of farm labor on the Dutch farms or a hazardous existence scratching for roots and hoping for game among the rapidly diminishing herds of the plains. The survivors merged with elements of the slave population to form the Coloured community of the present time. Though this group is now lumped together, it is far from homogeneous, even in the twentieth century. On the Cape Peninsula it is almost totally of slave background, with a long history in cities or coastal fishing communities. In the interior areas, it is much more predominantly Hottentot, and even slightly Bushman, in origin.

Slaves continued to be imported until 1767, though the Cape officials of the Company felt that there were already too many slaves in proportion to the number of colonists. The slaves were often guilty of heinous crimes (for which they were heinously punished) and were feared on account of their running "amok." Usually one-quarter to one-third of the slaves died on shipboard and of those who landed, one-third to one-half died within three months after their arrival at the Cape due to "despondency and change of climate and food." It is appalling to consider that while the Cape records contain many comments about the great loss to the Company, they say nothing about how these unfortunate, abused people themselves must have felt.[12]

In spite of the fact of slavery itself, in spite of the wretched conditions in which many slaves lived, and in spite of the apathy of much of the white population toward their spiritual welfare, the slaves were ripe for the ministry of such evangelicals as Van Lier and Vos. And within a few generations, through the work of missionaries from overseas and evangelical Christians of the Dutch churches, the Coloured population, with the exception of the Malay group, which has retained its Muslim worship to the present, became definitely Christian.

# II

# THE ARRIVAL OF MISSIONARIES

Early in the eighteenth century the pietist movement in Europe, especially in Germany, began to create interest in the unevangelized races of the world. On their way to India, the Danish missionaries Ziegenbalg and Plutschau stopped at the Cape, and were distressed by the condition of the Hottentots and the failure of the Dutch East India Company to bring the gospel to them. They wrote to Christians in Holland expressing this concern. Over a period of years, this led some of the ministers of the Classis of Amsterdam to become interested in finding a missionary to work among the Hottentots. Apparently no one with sufficient dedication and availability came forward in Holland, so a request was made to Count Zinzendorf and the Moravian brethren at Herrnhut, who had supplied missionaries for other far-off places.

## THE FIRST MORAVIAN MISSION: GEORGE SCHMIDT

George Schmidt had recently been released from an Austrian prison, where he had spent six years after being caught visiting and encouraging Protestants. At the time of his going to South Africa he was only twenty-seven years old, not ordained in any church, though a devout member of the *Unitas Fratrum,* the Moravian Brethren. He was not married. Schmidt first went to Amsterdam, where the Dutch Reformed divines examined him on doctrine and his missionary motivation; they declared themselves satisfied in both regards. The

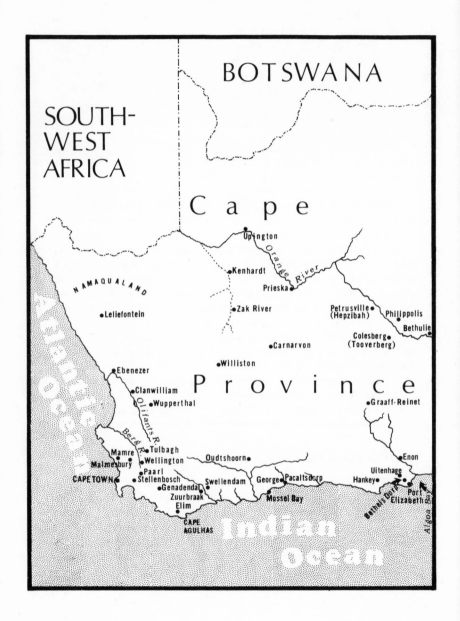

Company then sent Schmidt to the Cape on one of its ships, with a letter to the Governor stating that

> since the inclination of the aforesaid Schmidt is directed towards the pious object of, and may possibly be a blessed means for, leading the ignorant and uncivilized heathens to conversion, or at least to a more moral and better life, we have allowed him to proceed to you by this vessel, with the recommendation that you grant him every help and assistance in this good purpose.[1]

On arrival in Cape Town, Schmidt found a number of Christian people who were hospitable and encouraging. He met with the two ministers of the Dutch Reformed Church in Cape Town, but what passed between them is not recorded, though Schmidt did record in his diary that "One of them was of the opinion that we should commence with the Christians, and also raised the difficulty of the administration of baptism."[2]

In September, 1737, Schmidt left Cape Town for the site which had been allocated to him on the Sonderend River. This site, however, was not satisfactory to him, and less than a year later he moved farther down the Sonderend valley to Baviaanskloof. He wanted to be nearer a permanent Hottentot settlement and he feared being close to Company outposts, though his relations with the officer at the nearest outpost had been more than cordial — the sergeant in command had been led to a public profession of Christianity by Schmidt.

Schmidt wrote in his journal of the way of life he undertook:

> Every evening I visited the Hottentots, sat among them, distributed tobacco, and began to smoke with them. I told them that, moved by sincere love, I had come to make them acquainted with their Saviour, and to assist them to work. . . . I asked them if they knew that there was a great *Baas*, who had given them their cattle and all that they possessed.[3]

Afrika, one of the Hottentots who had accompanied Schmidt from Cape Town, answered that they acknowledged a creator whom they called Tui'qua. Schmidt then said, "Oh, dear people, this Tui'qua is our Saviour; He became man, and for us men He died upon the cross." Immediately after this section of the journal, Schmidt recorded this important decision:

> As soon as I had got my hut and garden into order, I attempted to master the Hottentot language, seeing that very

few of the Hottentots understand Dutch. They have three kinds of clicks, which I could not imitate; and I soon perceived that their language was too difficult for me to acquire. I therefore commenced to teach them to speak Dutch.[4]

Schmidt's life among the Hottentots was far from easy. He tried to teach them agriculture, but found them uninterested. But at least a few of the Hottentots were genuinely interested in his religious teaching. This success, rather than the difficulties, presented the real crisis for Schmidt's mission. Since he was not ordained he could not baptize his converts. The Dutch Reformed ministers in Cape Town expected him to present any candidate for baptism to them. Schmidt's reaction to this situation was to write to his brethren at Herrnhut for ordination. At about the same time (1739-1742), there was agitation in Holland about the orthodoxy of the Moravians. This was reflected at the Cape, and Schmidt feared that his work might suffer, that the approval of the Company and the local clergy might be withdrawn. He offered to submit his teaching and his pupils to examination by the ministers at Cape Town, but this offer was never accepted. In 1742 Schmidt received from Zinzendorf a paper stating that he was a fully ordained minister of the Moravian Brethren. On the trip back to Baviaanskloof, Schmidt baptized one of the converts and in the next few days five others, each in a nearby river.

The clergy of Cape Town objected strongly to Schmidt's action. He was called before the Governor, the Council of Policy, and the clergy. Their objections were these: 1) he was not a member of the Dutch Reformed Church; 2) his ordination was irregular because it was by letter rather than by the laying on of hands; and 3) he had baptized privately instead of in the church in the presence of the congregation. As a result of this trial Schmidt was refused permission to administer the sacraments until the case had been heard by the Classis of Amsterdam. This situation Schmidt found intolerable and as soon as he received from Herrnhut permission to leave, he left the Cape for Europe. His aim in returning to Europe was to obtain the permission necessary to carry on the work as he considered proper, but this was denied. He ended his days as a pastor in various parts of Central Europe.

There was general agreement at the Cape and in Holland that Schmidt's work should be carried on under the aegis of the Dutch Reformed Church, but this was never carried out. Where the responsibility for the failure of Schmidt's mission should lie is not fully clear. Probably there are a number of issues of personality that are lost in the mists of time. Some scholars have laid the blame on the colonists, most of whom were not eager to have their laborers baptized, a few of whom were even actively hostile. Others have blamed the Dutch Reformed clergy at the Cape, or distributed the blame between them and Schmidt himself, who might have been more humble and accepted their restrictions. Sectarian jealousies certainly existed. Perhaps the antagonism of the farmers has been exaggerated because of the unhappy experiences which Schmidt's successors at Baviaanskloof had with their farmer neighbors.

## THE SECOND MORAVIAN MISSION:  GENADENDAL

The Hottentots lost their land to the Dutch. Thus when the Moravians reopened the mission at Baviaanskloof in 1792 the Hottentots, by then a landless proletariat, were eager for a place to live, if not for receiving the benefits the mission had in mind to give them. Within a few months of their arrival they had sixty-one pupils in a school, a mission house built, and a garden started. The surviving reminders of Schmidt's mission were few: a pear tree he had planted and a Dutch New Testament in the possession of an ancient lady whom Schmidt had baptized. The old woman, Lena, could no longer read, but one other woman in the community apparently had been taught by one of Schmidt's pupils and could read the New Testament.

A number of factors had worked together to make it possible for the Moravians to reopen the mission. The establishment of a Lutheran Church in Cape Town indicated a more permissive attitude on the part of the Company toward other Protestant groups. In Holland the Moravians had become accepted as devout and orthodox Christians. At the Cape the evangelical spirit, exemplified especially by Van Lier, was making itself felt in the churches and among some of the Company officials. Johann Friedrich Reichel, a Bishop of the Moravians who had been in India, stopped at the Cape in 1787. Reichel was welcomed by Van Lier and his friends, and he in turn reported to the Brethren that it might again be possible to reopen the mission. The party which did reopen it was made up of three men, a Hollander and two Germans. Each had learned a trade, none were married, their ages ranged from thirty to forty-seven. They were all ordained as deacons before leaving Europe.

The rebuilding of the mission at Baviaanskloof, later named

Genadendal ("blessed valley" rather than "baboon gorge") dates the beginning of the permanent establishment of mission stations in South Africa. Though the men were married within a few years of their arrival, the Moravian village at Genadendal, and all the later stations, were actually monastic communities. Order was the keynote of life. All the missionaries ate together, prayed together, had fixed time for work, and fixed times for their private devotions. In church there were places for men, places for women, places for baptized, and places for the unbaptized; their graveyard also contained these divisions. Each of the missionaries had a trade, which he practiced, and which he taught to Hottentot boys who signed on as apprentices. Genadendal became especially famous for the manufacturing of knives, the only such factory in the Colony. The pattern of life which the Moravian missionaries knew was that of the peasant village, and this was the pattern they reproduced at Genadendal — frugality, hard work, and mystical devotion to the crucified Christ harmonized by the bell which governed the use of time.

Practically every traveller who left the environs of Cape Town stopped at Genadendal, and its hospitality was much appreciated by most, though the brothers themselves sometimes deplored the cost of this hospitality in both time and money. To many travellers Genadendal was the first evidence they met that Hottentots could become Christians; some became firm advocates of missions after such a visit. But others, unfortunately, saw in the institution only a barrier to the employment of Hottentots as farm laborers. If there were no such place as Genadendal, they reasoned, all Hottentots would be forced to work for the farmers all the time, and the farmers needed this labor.

Lady Anne Barnard, wife of the secretary of the Colony during the first British occupation, visited Genadendal in 1799. Here is her description of an evensong service:

> I doubt much whether I should have entered St. Peter's at Rome, with the triple crown, with a more devout impression of the Deity and His presence, than I felt in this little church of a few square feet, where the simple disciples of Christianity, dressed in the skins of animals, knew no purple or fine linen, no pride or hypocrisy. I felt as if I was creeping back seventeen hundred years, and heard from the rude and inspired lips of Evangelists the simple sacred words of wisdom and piety. The

service began with a Presbyterian form of psalm in a tone so sweet and loud, so chaste and true, that it was impossible to hear it without being surprised. The fathers, who were the sole music-masters, sang in their deep-toned bass along with them, and the harmony was excellent. This over, the miller took a portion of the Scripture and expounded it as he went along. The father's discourse was short, and the tone of his voice was even and natural, and when he used the words, as he often did, *myne lieve vriende,* "my beloved friends," I felt that he thought they were all his children.[5]

Visitors to Genadendal always described the place as one of tranquility, but the Brethren themselves did not always find it so, especially in the early years. A Moravian historian has listed the foes at Genadendal in 1793 as baboons, caterpillars, beetles, moles, gales, lack of milk and butter because of dry cows, sightseers, and visitors who expected cake and wine, demanded the best bedroom and often gave nothing for the hospitality they had received.[6] The Brethren also had trouble with the Stellenbosch church elders, who demanded that any converts should be baptized by the Stellenbosch predikant; but the Council of Policy upheld the right of the Moravians to baptize their own converts, though for a time they were refused permission to construct a church building and to ring their church bell, the cause of a long and acrimonious debate in the Colony. For a time, during the first decade, the Brethren were afraid that they might be attacked by their farmer neighbors. There is no doubt that the farmers' hatred of the missionaries and their work was real, but whether the threats of armed attack were ever anything but empty talk is impossible to ascertain.

In the long run, the relations of the Moravians with the officials of the Dutch East India Company were not of great importance, because the Company's rule in South Africa ended in 1795, and the same year the Company itself disintegrated, undermined by employees who retaliated for poor wages by myriad forms of corruption. The English immediately took the Cape from the Dutch in order to insure that their enemies, the French, would not get it.

The first British occupation lasted until 1803 when the Batavian Republic regained the Cape for a few years. But the Batavian Republic was nothing like the old Dutch East India Company; its leaders had been influenced by the ideas of the French Revolution. With the exception of a few of the more cosmopolitan people in

Cape Town, the Batavian Republic leaders and the English invaders were equally alien to the Dutch of the Cape. The Enlightenment had bypassed them. The industrial revolution might as well have been on another planet. Though they themselves were an outpost of empire, the interplay between East and West which was a by-product of the commercial empires had passed them by. Their eyes were on the interior of Africa, where hunting grounds and new grazing pastures attracted them. The British retook the Cape in 1806, and meant to keep it this time. Eventually this was bound to mean something to the Dutch colonists. Eventually the nineteenth century intruded upon their isolated way of life.

## THE LONDON MISSIONARY SOCIETY

Because of their close involvement in the question of race relations, missionaries have played an important role in the history of South Africa. One historian says that the arrival of the missionaries to the Hottentots was a greater shock to the Colony than all the changes in government between 1795 and 1806. Among the "race questions" plaguing South Africa, and continuing to do so, was the "Hottentot Question." This was peculiarly related to the missionaries of the London Missionary Society, and has merited them opprobrium in practically all South African history texts ever since. In fact, the word "missionary" said in a particular tone of voice in South Africa means a London Missionary Society missionary in the period from 1799 to about 1850. During that period the LMS had more, and more widely scattered, missionaries in South Africa than any other society. Furthermore, they had spokesmen who were from time to time able to be heard in the centers of decision-making, namely Parliament and the Colonial Office in London. For this last reason they were especially hated by some of the Dutch colonists, who felt that they had no way to influence the British colonial government.

While the missionaries may at times have seemed to the Dutch colonists a monolithic entity, they do not look that way from the perspective of the present day, and it is doubtful whether they often felt that way about themselves.

The LMS mission to South Africa began with a group of four missionaries who arrived in South Africa in March, 1799. They had had to brave the usual perils at sea and also unusual ones caused by the Napoleonic wars. The leader of the group was Dr. Johannes Theodorus Vanderkemp, a man in his fifties who, before he had been accepted as a missionary, had had widely varied experiences, both morally and vocationally. He was Dutch and had studied medicine and philosophy in Holland, as well as medicine in Edinburgh. His father had been a very learned pastor, considerably influenced by Pietism. For many years, however, Vanderkemp rejected this early evangelical training. But after his wife and daughter drowned and he nearly died himself in the same accident, he underwent a deeply emotional conversion experience, in which the personal reality of Jesus as Savior came to him as a direct confrontation. Throughout his life, in the periods of his anti-Christianity as well as in the periods of evangelical fervor, Vanderkemp was always an extreme individualist and a man of very strong convictions. His outspokenness often led to bad public relations — he even argued with the slave-owners of Cape Town that slave-owning is a sin against both God and man. Furthermore, he insisted that if it was right for him to preach to the Hottentots and bring them into the Christian fellowship, this was also the duty of all others who called themselves Christians. He did not expect the Boers to leave their farms as he had left Holland, but he did expect them not to impede his work and to contribute to its support. And he told them so. He always lived in the world of ideas. Near the end of his life Vanderkemp spent long hours in a mud hut writing a philosophical treatise on Paul's letter to the Romans. The other three men in the pioneer group were the Rev. J. J. Kicherer, also Dutch, Mr. James Edmonds, and Mr. William Edwards. Edmonds and Edwards were both British and both ordained after they arrived in South Africa, neither having had theological training. These two lasted in mission work no more than a year or so.

Three directions of mission work emanated from this early LMS group: the South African Society, with work in the Western Cape; Vanderkemp's efforts among both the Xhosa and the Hottentots in the Eastern Cape; and Kicherer's northward penetration, which involved first the Bushmen, then the Griquas, and finally the Batswana. It is important to note that the London Missionary Society was not only interdenominational in its supporters and agents, but was also international. In the early years of the work in South Africa, only a minority of the people sent out by the Society were British; the majority were Dutch and German, for whom language problems at the Cape were obviously less. Another factor was that academies for training missionaries had arisen in Germany, but no voluntary associations as sending agencies at this time except for the Moravians, while in Britain there were sending agencies but no training programs. The appointment of Vanderkemp led, before he left Europe for South Africa, to the founding of the Netherlands Missionary Society in Rotterdam. Soon after their arrival in Cape Town, the pioneers met together with evangelical-minded South Africans, those who had been influenced by the Rev. Mr. Van Lier and others. The Rev. M. C. Vos and Mrs. Mathilde Smith, who had already befriended the Moravians, became the leaders of the South African Society for Promoting the Extension of Christ's Kingdom which developed from the impetus of the arrival of the LMS missionaries. The first attentions of the new society were directed to the slaves in Cape Town, then to those in other parts of the Western Cape. The early years of the South African Society had many frustrations, meeting opposition from both the Batavian and the English regimes. This gradually disappeared, however, and general support increased, particularly in connection with the revival which was set off by an earthquake in Cape Town in 1809, which many interpreted as divine warning.

After a few weeks in Cape Town, where the missionaries met the Governor and the Fiscal, as well as church leaders, they set off for Roodezand (later known as Tulbagh). Here, in the church of which the Rev. M. C. Vos was the minister, Edmonds and Edwards were ordained. Vanderkemp and Edmonds went east to Graaff-Reinet. After securing wagons and supplies, Kicherer and Edwards went north to start a mission for the Bushmen on the Zak River.

## THE BUSHMAN AND GRIQUA MISSIONS

Who were the Bushmen? Today it is fairly well known that the Bushmen were the most aboriginal of the peoples inhabiting Southern Africa when the white men first arrived in the fifteenth century, though up until the nineteen century it was commonly thought that they were merely Hottentots who had been reduced to hunting and gathering life by the pressure of other population groups. Rock engraving and rock painting are to be found in many parts of Southern Africa, reminders that the Bushmen once roamed widely and, apparently, freely. But for the last two hundred years the Bushmen have been the hunted enemies of the whites, the Hottentots, and the Africans.

In the early years of the Dutch occupation, the Bushmen came openly to the Dutch, begging and stealing but never taking human life. Trouble began when the Dutch began to live in the interior, taking over the sources of water and driving away the game. The Bushmen were pushed more and more into the mountains until their food supply was exhausted and they were driven in desperation to stealing from the farmers. When the Company first gave the farmers permission to organize commandos against the Bushmen, each raid killed dozens of Bushmen, but as the Bushmen became more daring in their raids on Boer farms, the commandos began to kill hundreds of Bushmen at a time and distribute hundreds of Bushman children among themselves as "apprentices," usually apprenticed for life. These apprentices served as herdsmen for the farmers and they entered into the mixed bag of ancestors of the present-day Coloured people. In later years the need for farm labor, and thus for apprentices, became itself the justification for raids against the Bushmen. Through the first third of the nineteenth century, Bushmen had been numerous in the Eastern Cape and the Orange Free State, as well as Lesotho. But the pressure of white farmers from the south and west and of Africans from the east and north drove them into the most uninhabitable parts of the Drakensberg and Maluti mountains, where they were annihilated by the Basotho about the middle of the nineteenth century, when the Basotho had been hard pressed first by the Zulus, then by the Boers. In 1877 Bushmen were declared outlaws in the Kenhardt district and could legally be shot at sight by the police.

The Zak River area, to which Kicherer and Edwards went, was a desolate, arid region, except once every three or four years, when rain made the whole area a series of swamps. Kicherer has been charged with being "restless."[7] One wonders, however, when one notes how restless the farmers of the northern Cape have always been, whether it might not have been the climate of the place which caused such restlessness. Edwards was certainly no less restless. Within a year of the founding of the Zak River mission, Kicherer wrote, "Brother Edwards, wishing to teach the Hottentots his native English, left us to go a little farther into the country."[8] Further inland Edwards took up trading along with preaching and teaching. Eventually he gave up mission work altogether and concentrated on trading. Later he bought a farm in the Colony. Kicherer was not, however, left alone; for the first year or so, he was accompanied in his work at Zak River by Cornelius Kramer, a native of Tulbagh, who dedicated himself to mission work. Kicherer ended his connection with the London Missionary Society in 1806 when he took government employment as minister of the Dutch Reformed church at Graaff-Reinet. When Kicherer moved to Graaff-Reinet, it was necessary to close the Zak River mission, but some of the converts moved to Graaff-Reinet with Kicherer.

Kicherer found it difficult to establish "points of contact" for missionary teaching. This is hardly surprising considering the state of continuous warfare between the Dutch and the Bushmen. He wrote that the Bushmen,

> when approaching a white man for the first time, from some urgent motive, such as their ardent desire of obtaining a little tobacco, appear in an agony of fear, which discovers itself by the trembling of every limb; yet so vehement is their love of this narcotic, that they will venture anything to procure it; and had it not been for the powerful attraction of this favourite herb, which we liberally distributed among them, I am persuaded we could not have prevailed upon them to venture near us.[9]

Kicherer never learned the Bushman language, so what he learned of their thought was only through interpreters, Bushmen or Hottentots. His understanding of their religious views was that they knew of no divinity. Nor did they worship, he said, except in so far as they paid respect to an insect, the praying mantis, which they feared might cause them to be cursed if they hurt it. Occasionally they showed affection for their children − as do animals, Kicherer added. Under many circumstances the Bushmen killed or abandoned their children and the aged.[10]

> When we first entered upon our work, we laboured to convince our hearers by arguments addressed to their under-standings, but our endeavours in this way had little success. They continually raised objections and difficulties. We then resorted to another method; we insisted chiefly on the dying love of Christ, in the most simple and affectionate manner; we represented him as the all-sufficient friend of lost and helpless sinners; tenderly inviting them to give the fair trial of experience to our doctrine, by praying to Jesus. Since we

adopted this method, the Lord has been pleased to make the word effectual to many souls.[11]

A typical day in the first year of the mission:

Our days are spent in the following manner — About the time of the sun-rising we collect together for prayer, when we read the Scriptures and sing a hymn; then the elderly people depart, and the business of the school commences. We teach the younger people to spell and read Dutch. In the mean time our provision is prepared by a Boscheman [Bushman] girl. School being over, we proceed to our manual labour, such as gardening, building, etc. About noon we dine, and the afternoon passes away in the same occupations as the forenoon. Evening arriving, we conclude our day by prayer, singing hymns, and communication, in the plainest manner we know, the knowledge of divine things.[12]

Kicherer's relations with the neighboring farmers were apparently good. Floris Visser, the field-cornet for the northern border, had invited Kicherer to take up work there, had helped him get settled and had gotten the farmers of the area to contribute stock, especially sheep, to the mission. At Christmas time in 1799, several of the farmers went to Zak River to celebrate the Lord's Supper because it was so much closer than Tulbagh, the nearest Dutch Reformed church. Three years later, when the first converts were baptized, some of the farmers were also present.

On the third of October, 1802, I baptized four Hottentot men and two Hottentot women. On the preceding day they had given a satisfactory confession of our Calvinistic Creed, showing that they were well grounded in the pure word of God, and that they had found solid consolation in the truth, in confidence of which they could venture into the eternal world; declaring also that they were desirous by their walk and conversation, to shew forth the power of Jesus Christ. . . . The ordinance having been administered, the Apostolic benediction was pronounced over each of them, singly. The following Christians were witnesses of the sacred transaction: J. Scholz, C. Botma, Stephen Botma, Gerrit Maritz, and John van de Werhuisen. Service being over we had a Love-Feast together with our new brethren and sisters, being desirous to intimate that all the distinction which had before subsisted between them and us was now at an end, and that we should consider one another as members of Christ, supported by the same spiritual food. . . . The conversion of these poor heathen was scarcely so surprising to us, as the cordial union of so many Christians with us in these exercises, though so contrary to their former customs and prejudices.[13]

It is interesting to note that the firstfruits of the Bushman mission were not Bushmen but Hottentots. The nomadic habits of the Bushmen made it very difficult to retain them long enough to teach them. But then, too, the Hottentots knew some Dutch, so it is likely that they understood far more of what the missionaries were trying to teach. And one must remember the war of extermination which had been waged by the farmers against the Bushmen for about thirty years previously.

His only clearly visible success having been among the Hottentots, it is not surprising that Kicherer should have felt some attraction to work among them. To the north of the Zak River there were a variety of Hottentot groups. The Bastaards, later more politely known as the Griquas, were Hottentots with an infusion of European genetic material from wandering farmers, escaped soldiers and prisoners, hunters, and other stray Europeans. They had gradually been pushed northwards into the Orange River area. The Korannas (or Corannas) were more or less pure Hottentots who had withdrawn to the Orange River area and what became the Orange Free State before their tribal organization crumbled. Occasional hunters ventured north of the Orange River and communication between these varied groups and the Colony took place. Thus the Korannas had heard about the Zak River mission. The missionary wrote:

> Several of the Corannas [Korannas], from the Great, or Orange River, arrived at our Settlement about this time, repeating the invitation they had before sent to us, to remove to their country, which is about 300 miles distant, and preach the word of life among them. We held a Council with our old people, all of whom expressed their determination to follow us. Accordingly, we set out in May, 1801. Brother Anderson, who had joined us some months before, preceded us, with part of our property; Kramer, Scholtz, and myself followed at a distance with the bulk of the people. In the course of our journey we found the country far more populous than we had conceived.[14]

The result of this journey was the establishment of the mission station at Rietfontein (Reed Fountain), which was later moved to a more secure source of water, known first as Klaarwater and later as Griqua Town. Anderson continued in this area, working with the Griquas, as the people came to be known, until 1820 (at that time he moved to the coastal region east of Cape Town, Pacaltsdorp, and worked among the Cape Hottentots until his death in 1852).

Kicherer described the early work at Rietfontein:

> We built a long shed of Timber, Reeds, and Clay, the roof reaching to the ground. The middle part of it was our Church, at each end was a room, one of which was occupied by Brethren Anderson and Kramer, the other by myself and Brother Scholtz. The provisions were stored in my apartment. This building was appropriated to the worship of the Hottentots, another of similar construction was devoted to the instruction of the Corannas and Namaquas [another tribal group, mainly dwelling along the Atlantic Coast], whom we addressed by interpreters. Divine service was performed in both places at the same time, each of us officiating by rotation.[15]

Because they were hundreds of miles from anywhere that could supply provisions, vegetable planting was an important part of developing the station. For this, the missionaries needed to develop work habits in a people who were not at all accustomed to a life of planting and cultivating. It would appear that those whom Kicherer refers to as Hottentots were those who spoke Dutch and had moved from the Zak River with them. It would be interesting to know what understanding of the Christian faith these people held, who had the crucial task of interpreting to the Korannas and Namaquas.

Kicherer left Anderson and Kramer at Rietfontein and returned to the Zak River, and from there visited Cape Town once again:

> A convenient opportunity presenting itself at this time for a visit to the Cape, I gladly embraced it, as I had conceived a plan of forming a regular congregation of Hottentots, for which purpose I stood in need of a variety of articles, and particularly a good stock of clothes.[16]

Obviously the "missionary box" had not yet been instituted, but soon would be! The next year Kicherer returned to Europe because of ill health. While he was gone, the Zak River mission was continued by Christiaan Botma, a Dutch farmer who sold his farm to obtain provisions for the Bushmen. Botma was joined in 1805 by the

Rev. and Mrs. Arie Vos, new missionaries from Holland, sent out by the LMS.

During the first few years of the nineteenth century, the northwestern Cape was in a more or less constant state of fear, caused by the raids of a gang of half-breed cattle thieves who did not mind killing isolated farmers from time to time. Rumors began to spread that the LMS missionaries were organizing these brigands. In 1805 the Batavian government at the Cape sent a deputation north to investigate these rumors (they were always suspicious that the London Missionary Society was working for British interests in South Africa). The real reasons why the Zak River mission failed are probably impossible to determine. The government deputation, composed of Landdrost Van de Graaff and Dr. Lichenstein, placed the blame on the failure of the missionaries to require continued labor. One might also point to Kicherer's frequent jaunting to Cape Town and to the north; the resultant lack of consistent, persistent leadership may have been a serious drawback. Moffat, who arrived in South Africa in 1817, about a quarter of a century later, and who therefore cannot be counted an eyewitness, though he knew some of the same conditions in Namaqualand, felt that the Bushmen themselves were at fault in their refusal to live a settled life. This could be interpreted to mean that the whole enterprise was futile. Stow, who wrote even later, was a strong advocate of the Bushmen. His view was that the project was futile not because the Bushmen were incapable of change, but because the land was impossible to subsist upon.

The deputation did reveal a questionable aspect of missionary life, that of the trading enterprises undertaken by the missionaries. Trading, of course, is a wide area of human activity, particularly in a barter economy. A missionary was forced to become either a trader or a farmer, or, more likely, both. How much of the missionaries' time and energy went into the trading and whether he engaged in it beyond fulfilling his immediate needs are, of course, legitimate questions, but the data for answers is not available. One must also remember that the London Missionary Society sent out its first missionaries in the hope that they would quickly become self-supporting, so that the Society's funds could be used to transport others to the mission fields. When a salary was paid in those early years, it amounted to about thirty or forty pounds per year; five pounds was granted for materials with which to build a house. Even allowing for the difference in the value of money, these were very meager amounts. Under such circumstances it is not surprising that Kicherer and many other LMS missionaries took appointments in Dutch Reformed churches, where the stipend in a country parish was a hundred pounds a year.

While the early missionaries were at Zak River, a man named Stephanus arrived among them and offered his services to the mission. He was educated and clever with his hands, so the missionaries accepted his services. Some time later they received official notice and description of a clerk who had run away from Cape Town after having been guilty of forging money. When this notice was received, Stephanus quickly departed, before being recognized, and went north to the Orange River, to Kok's kraal (Griquas). Burchell, a traveller who visited the northern missions in 1811 wrote:

> He had with him a bible, given him at Zak River; and, with this in his hand, he set up as a missionary, and gained an ascendancy over the minds of the kraal, such as, the missionaries have confessed, they have never been able to gain. He persuaded them to attend to agriculture, and also to erect a church. This he built in a superior style; and, conducting the religious services with such imposing formality and ceremony, made his hearers at length believe that he was expressly sent to them from heaven. He preached such doctrines as suited his purpose, and was not suspected of imposition, even when, on desiring to take on another wife in addition, he declared he had the divine command for selecting such and such a female. At last, on some occasion he made a journey into the country of the Great Namaquas, and was murdered by the natives. When the missionaries afterwards attached themselves to the Kok's and Barends' party, they had great difficulty in persuading them that Stephanus was nothing but an imposter; so successfully had he managed to secure an authority over their minds, as well as over their conduct.[17]

During the few years immediately after the Zak River mission closed, there was no missionary effort specifically for the Bushmen. But since the Hottentots, Griquas, and Namaquas were much more responsive, personnel were free to develop mission communities for these people. Occasionally a few Bushman families joined these communities, but this was only sporadic and haphazard. Not until

1814 was another organized effort made on behalf of the Bushmen. This was in an area to the east of the Zak River, just south of the Orange River. Two mission stations (missionary "institutions" in the language of the time) were established, one called Tooverberg (or Thornberg or Grace Hill), which was located where the town of Colesberg is now, and the other called Hephzibah, near where the present village of Petrusville is. These places were established with the approval of the secretary of the Colony, Colonel Bird, though they were outside the boundaries of the Colony. Within a few months there were several hundred people living at the two stations. This very success, however, in attracting the Bushmen undid the enterprise. Farmers in the district claimed that such an assemblage of "savages" was a danger to the Colony. They also complained that the "tame" Bushmen who worked on their farms were running away and seeking asylum at the mission stations; moreover, they said, it was difficult to obtain Bushmen as herdsmen if they had the option of living at a mission station.

Neither of the men in charge of these missions was an ordained missionary. Erasmus Smit, who was in charge at Tooverberg, had been born in Holland and had previously served at Bethelsdorp. The man in charge of Hephzibah was William Corner, a product of the London Missionary Society mission on Dememaraland (British Guiana), and a Negro; he too had served at Bethelsdorp. Both were given notice in 1818 that they must close down the stations and move within the Colony, the farmers' wishes winning out.

Very soon after Smit had left Tooverberg, Dutch farmers had taken over the land, and the town of Colesberg grew up around the water supply which had formerly served the mission. Title to the land was given to the Dutch Reformed Church, which acquired money for its local purposes by selling town lots. At Hephzibah, the Bushmen remained for some time, but eventually were driven out by the continual plundering of the Korannas. As the farmers moved closer to them, they moved farther into the recesses of the mountains, in what is now Lesotho. Some accepted life on the farms and became "tame" Bushmen.

At Philippolis and Bethulie, north of the Orange River, attempts were made again to create missionary Bushman communities, but the antipathy between the Griquas and the Korannas and the Bushmen, as well as the rapid movement of the Dutch farmers into the southern Orange Free State area during the 1820's and 1830's, frustrated these efforts. The last effort of the London Missionary Society was made during the 1840's when a Bushman captain named Madura asked the missionaries at the Kat River to send teachers to his people. Several Hottentot Christians answered this call and went to live with Madura's people, teaching them agriculture as well as Christianity. The work was going well until the outbreak of the war of 1846-47. During the war, Madura and his people helped the government troops by scouting and serving in the Hottentot regiments, but after the war their land was incorporated in the Colony and each man was required to pay one pound a year in taxes. This was utterly impossible, but the objections of the missionaries on their behalf were useless, and so, for failure to pay the tax, they lost the right to live where they had always lived. They, too, were faced with the choice of living as landless farm tenants or fleeing to the Drakensberg mountains. The chief and his family chose the latter, but some of his people chose the former and were absorbed into the Hottentot, then Coloured, group.

# III

# DR. VANDERKEMP

While Kicherer and Edwards were travelling north to begin their work among the Bushmen, Vanderkemp and Edmonds were travelling east to start a mission among the Xhosa people beyond the eastern boundary of the Colony. The decision to divide their resources was made by the group in Cape Town. An invitation had come from some Bushman clans, and Kicherer felt that such a clear call should be heard and answered. Vanderkemp was more interested in a grand strategy, believing that to work among the Xhosas was to open the whole continent of Africa for the progress of the gospel. Beyond these reasons, it had become clear already in Cape Town that the men were unable to work closely as a team; perhaps, it was thought, the division into two groups was a way out of this predicament. At any rate, because of this decision, there were within a very few years mission stations over a large part of southern Africa.

Vanderkemp and Edmonds travelled from Cape Town to Graaff-Reinet. At Graaff-Reinet the landdrost attempted to dissuade them from their goal by telling them of the war going on between the Xhosas and the colonists and of the rebellion of some colonists against the British. Obviously these were troubled times. Vanderkemp was not deterred, but Edmonds began to worry, wondering whether the Lord was not really calling him to missionary service in India. Some of the colonists begged Vanderkemp and Edmonds to stay within the Colony and minister to them, but Vanderkemp saw this as one of the devil's lures to keep them from spreading the

44

gospel among the Xhosas. After some delays, Ngqika (Gaika), foremost chief of one of the Xhosa groups (not of all the Xhosas, as the British and Dutch thought), gave permission for them to come to his headquarters. Ngqika's home was not always in the same place, but his territory generally was southeast of the Winterberg mountains, inland from what is now King William's Town.

Vanderkemp was the first missionary to go to the Xhosa people, but he was far from the first white man. Hunters and cattle buyers had visited these people from time to time for nearly a hundred years. When he arrived, there were perhaps as many as a dozen white men living outside the Colony, pasturing their animals among those of the Xhosas and trading in a variety of things, not all of them legal (guns and ammunition were, of course, the most desirable items of trade, for which a Xhosa chief would pay well in cattle). These men were helpful to Vanderkemp to the extent that they understood Xhosa and could help him learn the protocol necessary to get things from a chief, to buy food, etc.; but they were a distinct liability in the sense that Vanderkemp ran the risk of being identified with them, men whose example was anything but Christian. On the other hand, the traders had reason to fear Vanderkemp, since most of them were wanted in the Colony for deserting the army or for various other crimes. A preacher poking among them was not at all attractive. What role these men actually played in Ngqika's ambiguous attitude toward Vanderkemp is impossible to discern positively, but it seems likely that in the main they did not make his way easier.

Vanderkemp arrived among the Xhosas in September, 1799, and late in October Ngqika granted him a site. On January 1st, 1800, Edmonds left, having finally concluded that his call was really to the people of Bengal. During that year Vanderkemp began preaching and teaching. Not many Xhosas showed any permanent interest in his message, and after a time they were forbidden to attend his meetings by Ngqika. But some Hottentot women who were married to Xhosa men did become faithful listeners and eventually felt the power of conversion. And when Vanderkemp found it necessary to move, as he did more than once, these followers managed to continue to meet with him. In fact, when he was forced to move back into the Colony, about May, 1801, some of these people went with him.

The failure of Vanderkemp's mission to the Xhosas must be seen against the background of the turmoil of southeastern Africa. The rebellion of Graaff-Reinet by Dutch farmers who hated the authority of both the Dutch and the English was a small thing, but symptomatic of similar movements that would come later. Among the Xhosa people, there were serious difficulties between Ngqika and his uncle, Ndlambe, who had been regent during Ngqika's minority and attempted to continue to act as paramount chief. This led to several pitched battles, many skirmishes, and much subversive activity between the followers of the two men. And it created a wonderful atmosphere for the scheming activities of some of the renegade whites who came to live among the Xhosas.*

Farther north, in Zululand, a larger dislocation had begun late in the eighteenth century. There, apparently, the population had become too great for the water and grass resources of the area and the usual solution to this, migration, was no longer possible because the extremity of the continent had been reached on the east and south and the European settlers barred the way to the west. New methods of warfare, perhaps inspired by contact with Europeans, also upset traditional balances. A three-way struggle between the Ndwandwes, the Ngwanes, and the Mtetwas prepared the way for the eventual mastery of large sections of southeastern Africa by Tshaka, a Zulu who managed to consolidate the gains of his Mtetwa overlord, Dingiswayo. The reverberations of Tshaka's tyranny were felt as far north as Lake Tanganyika and as late as the second half of the nineteenth century, though Tshaka himself died in 1828. Refugees from the disturbances in Zululand pushed their way south and pressed upon the Xhosas and their neighbors just at the time that they were already being pressed from the west by the whites. This was the general situation in which Vanderkemp had attempted to establish a mission.

When Vanderkemp was forced to return to Graaff-Reinet because of Ngqika's unfriendliness, he had with him a number of Hottentot followers, and this number rapidly increased. At the Dutch Reformed Church in Graaff-Reinet, he held services for as many as two hundred Hottentots, until the whites of the town protested so

*The British throughout Ngqika's lifetime took the view that Ngqika was paramount chief and that he had sufficient power to bring his people into line if only he wanted to; it is very doubtful that he did have power over any more than a portion of the Xhosa people at any time. His influence became even less after he got help from the British to fight against Ndlambe in 1819.

loudly that the services had to be held elsewhere. Vanderkemp also started a school for these people. At this time, there were many Hottentots in Graaff-Reinet and in the bush near the Sundays River because many had run away from farms where they had been working when the farmers rebelled against the government. Some Hottentots had fought with the Xhosas against the whites, and this had brought retaliation against the Hottentots by the farmers, even though the farmers were anxious to retain their services as herdsmen. The Hottentots had sought protection from Maynier, the landdrost (magistrate), whose "softness" toward the non-whites had been one of the causes of the rebellion. These refugees were near at hand and eager for the attention which Vanderkemp gave them. In fact, two new recruits from the LMS, the Rev. James Read and the Rev. A. A. Vanderlingen, had already started to work among these people when Vanderkemp returned from Ngqika's country.

Later in 1801 the disturbances in Graaff-Reinet got worse and Vanderkemp received permission to go to Algoa Bay (present-day Port Elizabeth) with those Hottentots who wished to live with him. One hundred and nine Hottentots left Graaff-Reinet with Vanderkemp and Read in February, 1802; some deserted along the way and seventy-seven arrived at Algoa Bay. The government had promised a grant of land for a missionary institution (something like Genadendal was doubtless in their minds). This was not given, however, until 1804, when the government had reverted to Dutch hands. In the meantime, Vanderkemp and his followers had shifted from one farm to another, with some very unpleasant run-ins with their Dutch farmer neighbors on occasion. These farmers, like their cousins near Genadendal, feared that the institution would make it impossible for them to obtain labor on any terms they considered reasonable.

When Vanderkemp and Read left Graaff-Reinet, Vanderlingen stayed on and continued to preach and teach among the Hottentots there, even though the Boers objected strongly that it was not right to teach Hottentots to read and write and thus make them "equal to the Christians," meaning themselves. Several other missionaries had arrived in the first few years of the nineteenth century: Tromp, Manenburg, Verster, and Bakker, all of whom were Dutch. They worked among the slaves in various districts of the western Cape, emphasizing the establishment of schools, as well as of churches.

The Peace of Amiens in Europe (1802) meant that the English left the Cape and the Dutch returned. However, it was not the government of the Dutch East India Company that returned, but rather the representatives of the Batavian Republic, the pro-French government of Holland during the Napoleonic period. As might be expected of a republican government born out of the influence of the French Revolution, the Batavian regime at the Cape was revolutionary in many respects. It was headed by two men, Commissioner de Mist, whose job was to set up the structure of government for the Colony, and Governor Janssens. Each man made a long tour of the country and each left a record of his views on what South Africa needed, even though the Batavian regime was too short-lived to change either the political or the social structure.

Governor Janssens met Vanderkemp at Algoa Bay in 1803. De Mist had approved of the British governor's stated intention to make a grant of land for Vanderkemp's mission. To choose the site, Janssens appointed a committee of four Boers, three of whom were local officials and farmers, plus James Read. The place they chose was the one since known as Bethelsdorp, a large tract of land with a tributary of the Zwartkops River flowing through it when it happened to have rained. The relationship of the missionaries to the farmers had never been good, and they certainly were not helped by Vanderkemp's officiating at the marriage of Read and a Hottentot girl, soon after the allotment of the Bethelsdorp grant. Matters were not helped, either, by the inclination of the missionaries to believe the worst of the farmers about their treatment of their Hottentot laborers.

Theal's description of Dr. Vanderkemp's meeting with Commissioner de Mist, with whom he had gone to school in Holland thirty-five years before, is the basis of the general South African view of Vanderkemp and missions in general:

> Dr. Vanderkemp was dressed in coat, trousers, and sandals; but was without shirt, neckcloth, socks or hat. In a burning sun he travelled about bareheaded and thus strangely attired. Yet his conversation was rational, and his memory was perfectly sound. He had formed an opinion that to convert the Hottentots to Christianity it was necessary to descend in style of living to their level, to be their companion as well as their teacher, and being thoroughly earnest he was putting his views into practice.

> ...The missionaries themselves were living in the same manner as the Hottentots, and were so much occupied with

teaching religious truths that they entirely neglected temporal matters.[1]

Poor Dr. Vanderkemp might better have lived in the twentieth century, when living on the same level as the people is applauded, even if seldom done.

The barrenness of the land at Bethelsdorp soon became obvious: the only thing productive about it was a salt pan, which, when the city of Port Elizabeth grew up nearby, became a source of income for some of the people. To this day, the place is still a desolate stretch with little besides rocks and aloes, although it will soon be so covered with houses for the coloured industrial workers of Port Elizabeth that even the aloes will probably be gone. It was unfortunate that Read, as a member of the committee to choose the site, was so completely ignorant of the agriculture in South Africa at that time. There has always been a suspicion that the site chosen was meant to make it impossible for the Hottentots to make a go of farming for themselves, thus forcing them to hire themselves out to the local farmers. Dr. Vanderkemp sent all of his inheritance, £ 137 per year, keeping the people from Bethelsdorp from starving. When the British settlers arrived in 1820, making Port Elizabeth an important seaport, many Hottentots from Bethelsdorp became transport riders and managed to make a living in that way, though such an itinerant mode of life made it difficult for the mission to instruct the men.

Though it may be true that teaching the Hottentots to be industrious was not Dr. Vanderkemp's primary aim, it is not true that he was not concerned at all about this area of life. In 1806 and 1807 he and Read were joined at Bethelsdorp by Mrs. Mathilde Smith, a South African lady who had been one of the founders of the South African Society. She had twice been widowed and all her children had died, so she devoted her time and money to mission work, not only at Bethelsdorp, but for many years in Cape Town. Her relations with Vanderkemp, though long and cooperative (she was at his bedside when he died), were marred by her ownership of slaves. Mrs. Smith taught the women and children at Bethelsdorp many of the domestic skills they needed for a settled life, and one of these, knitting socks and nightcaps, became a commercial enterprise when these were sold to the military personnel in the Eastern Cape. And besides the knitting, Bethelsdorp soon became engaged in the following economic activities: grazing, charcoal-burning, lime-burning, soap-boiling, fishing, smithy, wagon repair, turning, wagon driving, salt mining, and making mats and baskets. The charge commonly made in South African history texts, then, that the LMS missionaries were not sufficiently "practical" does not seem wholly justified, if at all.

What really created a bad public image for the Bethelsdorp missionaries, and a few of the other LMS missionaries, was their marriage to non-whites. Read married a Hottentot girl from Bethelsdorp and Vanderkemp, several years later, married the daughter of a Malagasy slave woman, both of whom he emancipated. Dr. Lichenstein, who accompanied de Mist, wrote cynically of Read:

> This man, in order to give a striking proof of his lowliness and humility, had married a young Hottentot woman belonging to the establishment. The girl was baptized a few days before her marriage; but neglected as she was by him, both personally, and with regard to the formation of her mind, nobody could be made to believe that he married her at all from inclination.[2]

Whatever Read's motives in marriage, there are many recorded statements by people who visited the Reads in later years which attest to their Christian home and family. Three of Read's sons became missionaries of the LMS.

Though the Batavian officers had granted the site for Bethelsdorp, their relations with the missionaries were not cordial. After his tour of the Colony, de Mist ordered that no new missionaries would be permitted at Genadendal, Bethelsdorp, or the Zak River, nor could any new mission stations be established within the Colony. Outside the Colony the missionaries could teach, but they were to have no contact with the colonists. This was because the Dutch were afraid that the missionaries were British sympathizers, or even British agents. This suspicion grew until the British retook the Cape in 1806; in 1805, in fact, Vanderkemp had been called to Cape Town on this charge and was not permitted to return to Bethelsdorp. In that year, too, Janssens issued regulations for Bethelsdorp stating 1) that no missionary at Bethelsdorp could go beyond the bounds of the Colony, 2) that no Hottentot who was already working for a farmer could be admitted at Bethelsdorp (only those who had never been employed or those who had been admitted to the station prior to the new regulations), and 3) that while reading could be taught, writing could not. In his report to the home government, Janssens summed up his view of missionaries as follows:

> If the harm that missionaries have done in the Colony and its
> surroundings (with the exception of the Moravian Brethren in
> Genadendal) is weighed against the good they have done, it
> will be found that the harm is very serious and the good
> amounts to nil. Most of these missionaries (rogues) should be
> sent away with the greatest possible haste, and those who may
> be allowed to stay − if there are any − should be given
> entirely new instructions.[3]

It is not surprising that the missionaries rejoiced at the return of the
British in 1806. Even the Dutch at the Cape were not unhappy to
see ousted such radical reformers as had allowed freedom of worship
to Roman Catholics and Muslims and had planned to turn education
over to secular authorities. The Batavians were not popular at all
with the conservative Dutch of the Cape.

The daily life at Bethelsdorp included daily worship as well as
Sunday worship. In the first years Vanderkemp and Read had led all
the services, but when converts had been made and trained, these,
too, preached and prayed in the services. The worship was often
emotional and got longer and longer until, in 1809, when daily
sermons were approaching two hours in length, a limit of half an
hour of preaching on weekdays and an hour on Sunday was
established. As members of the community went out to work on
various farms for the whites, they preached to their fellow workers
in these places. Occasionally they were flogged by the farmers for
this missionary activity, but nevertheless, groups of learners and
worshipers developed throughout the district. Vanderkemp itiner-
ated from time to time to teach these new converts and also to
preach occasionally to the one or two pockets of tribal Hottentots
still living in the bush areas of the river valleys. It is interesting to see
how Vanderkemp taught when he spent a week with one of these
groups who had never heard the gospel. The pattern of his teaching,
on one occasion at least, was this: incarnation, Jesus' struggle with
the scribes and Pharisees, Jesus' temptation, baptism, beatitudes,
healing, betrayal, crucifixion, burial, and story of the rich young
ruler (regeneration). This is an interesting contrast to the more
common missionary pattern beginning with the nature of God and
creation. No doubt the emphasis on Jesus' struggles against the
powers of this world was, in part at least, a reflection of
Vanderkemp's own temporal situation. Or perhaps his own intran-
sigence, as his white neighbors saw it, was a result of his theology.

Dr. Vanderkemp died in Cape Town in 1811, on just the day when, in London, the Directors of the London Missionary Society were appointing him superintendent of the South African Mission. He had been in poor health for some time. It is doubtful whether he could possibly have acted effectively as superintendent because of his almost complete estrangement from the South African white public. His relations with his missionary colleagues were not the best, either. Mr. Pacalt, a missionary at Bethelsdorp wrote: "Everything which he does not approve of he accounts as coming from the devil. But one must be silent, because Dr. Vanderkemp is old."[4] Vanderkemp's biographer summarized him thus:

> Always he appears as a man whose inner life was lived either in strong light, or in deep shadow. It had no half-tones. In matters of faith and in judgment of men and affairs his convictions were sharp and definite. As in his youth, so in the entire history of his soul he was one who lived dangerously — venturing wholly upon the unseen for support and guidance, and accepting, perhaps too readily, the vivid colours of first impressions. . . . Even when contending for civil and religious liberty, he allowed little freedom for others to state their case.[5]

At the time of his death Vanderkemp had been engaged in collecting evidence for and presenting to the government a long list of cases in which Hottentot farm servants had been mistreated, injured, and, in some cases, killed by Boer farmers. Vanderkemp felt that he had not received satisfaction from the local magistrate about these charges, so he took them to the governor, and a circuit court was to hear the cases. This did happen in 1812, Read carrying the burden of pushing the charges. This court is known in South African history as the "Black Circuit" because of the feeling of the Boer farmers that it was an ignominious affair that any "Christian," as the Boers called themselves, should have to justify his conduct in relation to his non-white servants. Some of the cases brought judgments against the farmers, some acquittals, but the large majority fell away for lack of evidence.

Dr. Vanderkemp has long been tagged eccentric. The Afrikaner historians have at least done him the honor of making him a villain. He might be an appropriate hero-saint for that tiny group of rebels among South African students and young people who want integration and a new deal in politics for the non-white population.

# IV

# THE EXPANSION OF
# HOTTENTOT MISSIONS

In spite of the antipathy of the farmers and the scepticism of the government, the missionary institutions grew in number, almost from year to year. In 1807 the Moravians received a grant of land in the Malmesbury district for an institution named Mamre. This was an area where the remnant of an old Hottentot tribe lived, and these people became the inhabitants of the mission. In 1815 the Moravians were granted another site — Enon, on a tributary of the Sundays River. It had a difficult time for it was destroyed by the Xhosas in 1819; but was rebuilt afterwards. Elim, a Moravian institution near Cape Agulhas, was founded in 1825. At the same time, the Moravians were asked to take over the leper settlement in the Caledon district, which the government had established a few years earlier under the direction of the local Dutch Reformed minister. The name of the place was "Hemel en Aarde" (Heaven and Earth); from all descriptions it appears that its aspect was more that of "Aarde" than that of "Hemel."

The London Missionary Society was also acquiring new institutions during this period. The Caledon Institution at Zuurbrak was started in 1811. Pacaltsdorp, just west of George, grew out of contacts that Read made with a small group of Hottentots still living under their chief when he was in George for the sitting of the circuit court in 1812 (the Black Circuit). Theopolis was founded as a place for the overflow from Bethelsdorp. It was near the ocean in the vicinity of what is now Port Alfred; it was a much more fertile site, but was on the path of the Xhosa incursions into the Colony and was often attacked. It was established not so much out of the government's generosity towards the Hottentots as out of the desire to have a buffer between the colonists and the Xhosas. The land at Theopolis had been occupied by Xhosas until the government pushed them all east of the Fish River.

All of these institutions were primarily for the Hottentots – or Coloured people, as they were rapidly becoming by the intermixture of slave and white people with the indigenous Hottentots and Bushmen. But as early as 1808 there were some Xhosas living at Genadendal. Mamre also had some Xhosas, as well as some Damara people, from as far north as what is now South West Africa. These Damaras had come seeking missionaries to go to their own country. Later, in the 1830's, there were Fingoes (Zulu refugees) and Batswana living at Theopolis and other institutions in the Eastern Cape.

## DR. PHILIP AND THE LONDON MISSIONARY SOCIETY

During the decade 1810 to 1820, the LMS in South Africa had a difficult time. Some of the missionaries were accused of immorality, and this combined with the stories of missionaries who had married Hottentot women (doubtless in some minds marrying a Hottentot woman was an act of immorality in itself) and the Black Circuit gave the missionaries a very bad public image. Some new recruits when they had just arrived in Cape Town were drawn into public criticism of their LMS colleagues even before they had met them. Some of these withdrew from the mission society and took positions as Dutch Reformed pastors. All this eventually caused the LMS in London to send the Rev. John Campbell to observe the situation and report back, and the Rev. John Philip to act as superintendent of the Society in South Africa.

Philip became the best known – in fact the most hated – missionary of the LMS. He served as superintendent from 1819 until his death in 1851, though he was not able to do much the last few years. When Philip arrived in South Africa he was not a young man. He had already served as pastor of several congregations in Britain. He very early met the attitude, still prevalent, that "you can't understand South Africa unless you were born here." But the real reasons why he was so widely disliked by many white South

Africans were that he was responsible for the establishment of legal equality for non-whites with whites in the Cape Colony, that he assisted the campaign against slavery in the British Parliament by supplying information about the South African situation, and that he opposed the expansion of white landholding, which robbed non-whites of the lands they had traditionally held. Many people of his time and most people since have considered Philip a political meddler who should have stuck to his missionary business. His reply was that the missionary task included helping a person meet his basic needs — for the Hottentots and slaves the right to sell their labor in a fair market for the best available price and for the Bantu the right to sufficient land for a subsistence for themselves and their children.

Professor Macmillan, a historian who has written two important works on South African history based on the Philip papers, and who is one of Philip's few admirers, claims that Philip had a right and an obligation to express his views on South African affairs, especially frontier matters, because he was far better informed about what was going on in the country and on its borders than most people, even government officials. He regularly travelled to all the mission stations of the LMS, which at that time were scattered throughout the Colony and beyond its eastern and northern boundaries, and he received regular reports of events from those stations. Thus he was in a unique position for suggesting and criticizing policies. Philip was an early advocate of the current idea that a Christian must attempt to influence events by making an informed witness at the centers of decision-making. His despair was that what he felt most necessary was not done, because the primary interest of the Colonial Office in Britain was to curtail expenditure. He would have liked the kind of colonial administration with subsidized education and medical services that came about in central Africa in the twentieth century. The irony of Philip is that some of the things he is blamed for are not what he advocated at all but were the policies of the Colonial Office in spite of his protests. He had more influence on a small group of humanitarian-minded men in South Africa, especially in Cape Town, who were to manage to keep the policy of legal equality alive, at least in the Cape, for more than a hundred years before it was drowned by Afrikaner nationalism in the middle of the twentieth century.

Philip's first foray into politics was in support of the claims of the 1820 settlers. His next arose from his observations of the

Hottentots on the mission stations and on the farms. Some of them were keen to improve their standard of living and develop skills that would be useful to the community; but the laws of the Colony made it very difficult for them to leave the employ of a farmer or move to a new district to seek work. Not being slaves, they were not automatically fed and housed and taken care of in their old age, but they did not have very much more freedom than a slave in many situations. If a Hottentot child lived with his parents on a farm, the farmer had the right to the child's services from the age of eight till eighteen as recompense for the food the farmer had provided. If a Hottentot was travelling without permission and without proof of employment, he was likely to be declared a vagrant and required to work for a farmer whom the magistrate named. Thus the mission stations were considered by the Hottentots as centers of refuge, even if they were as barren as Bethelsdorp. Philip, being a Whig, as were most nonconformists of his time, believed that the free exchange of goods and services was the system most likely to lead to justice all round. But unless the Hottentots could claim the same legal protection from the courts as whites, they could not sell their labor freely. Therefore he pressed for Ordinance 50 of 1828, which said that no law could be passed which differentiated between free (non-slave) people on the basis of race. When the Cape Colony received parliamentary government several decades later, the franchise rights were nonracial — few non-whites could meet the property qualifications, but it was not *race* which barred them from voting. At times, enough Coloureds had the right to vote in some constituencies to make a significant difference in the policies followed by their Members of Parliament. If *this* was a bad thing then Philip quite rightly should be blamed.

The same group of men who supported Philip on rights for Hottentots also advocated the emancipation of slaves. When emancipation was passed by the British Parliament in 1833, Philip was again blamed, especially by those frontier farmers who felt he had undue influence with the Colonial Office. This was one of the reasons they left the Colony in the Great Trek of 1836-1846.

## GRIQUA MISSIONS

The work among the Griquas centered around Griqua Town in the west and Philippolis in the east (in what is now the Orange Free

State). During the 1820's the Griquas at Griqua Town had an unpleasant time, with quarreling between the new leadership which followed the ways of the missionaries, and the old tribal leaders. Finally Adam Kok, the tribal leader, moved off to the east (where the missionaries established themselves at Philippolis in order to stay within reach of him), and Nicholas Waterboer, a young man who had been trained as a teacher by the missionaries, became the new chief of Griqua Town (Waterboer was despised by some of the Griquas because he was part Bushman). From the early 1830's on, the constant intrusion of white farmers who wanted land, and traders whose sales from their brandy wagons drove the Griquas into debt and thus forced them to sell their land, made what had earlier seemed a promising mission venture into a rearguard action merely to hold the communities together. The Philippolis community sold out completely to the Boers of the Free State. During the 1860's the people of this community trekked east to Griqualand, a stretch of land just under the Drakensberg Mountains, between the Transkei and Natal. Eventually they lost most of their land there as well, to white farmers, leaving little more than the Griqua National Church and the name Kokstad as a reminder of better days.

The kind of Christianity introduced among the Griqua people placed great emphasis on education, the aim of which was to enable them to read the Scriptures. Musical instruments and dancing were forbidden as the work of the devil. Burchell, a traveller who visited Klaarwater (Griqua Town) in 1812, wrote that the aim of the missionaries was a "serious" people. Burchell also reported that at the time he visited them, the missionaries were having a very uphill fight against polygamy; the preponderance of women in the community, he said, meant that neither men nor women preferred monogamy. Nevertheless, some of the people had submitted to the rule the missionaries imposed.

About 1820, the Rev. William Anderson of Griqua Town got in trouble with Lord Somerset because he refused to recruit soldiers for the Colony. Anderson was expected to secure the peace of the Colony by promoting a stable society beyond it. In return for these benefits the governor gave occasional food supplies and permission for the mission to exist beyond the borders of the Colony. In the 1820's Mr. John Melville, who had held a high-paying post as government surveyor, accepted the post of government agent at Griqua Town in order to try to establish order there and bring some harmony to the relations between the missionaries, the Cape government, and the Griquas. In a few years Melville gave up in despair and became a regularly appointed missionary of the LMS.

In 1834 Nicholas Waterboer, accompanied by the Rev. Peter Wright, went to Cape Town for the festivities in connection with the emancipation of the slaves. The colonial authorities were impressed with Waterboer and they signed an agreement with him in December of that year. By this treaty he agreed to preserve order in his territory, to return to the Colony any criminal or fugitive who sought refuge, and to assist the colonial government in eliminating the robber groups who lived on the islands of the Orange River. In return, Waterboer was to receive a hundred pounds in money, two hundred muskets and ammunition, fifty pounds sterling for the mission school, and salary for a government agent. The Rev. Wright was appointed government agent.

In 1811 there were about 800 inhabitants of Griqua Town; by about 1825 there were about 3,000 people in the area and by 1842 there were about 4,800. But by about 1840 there were signs that the all-important spring was drying up, and this eventually happened. Griqua Town disappeared as an important mission station and stop on the route to the interior. Not all the people at Griqua Town were Griquas. There were also Korannas, some Bushmen, and Batswana. By this same time nearly all the Griquas were literate, but this was not true of the other groups; nearly 300 adults and about 800 children attended school.

The Griquas west of the Vaal River kept their independence until the time of the discovery of diamonds, about 1870. After much dispute, the territory was declared to belong to Waterboer's Griquas. But they were completely unable to control the shanty towns of miners who had come from all over the world to seek their fortunes, so they turned over their claim to the British government, which added Griqualand West to the Cape Colony. Many Griquas went to work at the diamond mines. Others continued their pastoral pursuits, moving west as the whites took over their lands, or becoming farm hands on the white-owned farms. By this time, the end of the nineteenth century, these people were decidedly Christian in their outlook, and their churches were the centers of their community life. Some had become Anglicans, Catholics, and Methodists, but to this day many still cling to the "Independency" of the London Missionary Society and are a part of the United Congregational Church.

During the first three-quarters of the nineteenth century, the missionaries to the Griquas and others in the Orange River valley made valiant efforts to irrigate the land. Their purpose was to create stable communities where their teaching could be continuous. In many of the areas that are now being bulldozed for massive dams and irrigation schemes, the LMS missionaries used what tools they had to dig out water furrows for farming. Occasionally, years of hard work were fruitless because the calculations had been wrong. But more often difficulties arose after some good years of effective irrigation: increasing over-grazing caused a change in the vegetation, and leached-out soil became badly eroded. Conservation methods are now the biggest need. The charge that the missionaries were not practical and were interested only in the souls, not the bodies, of their converts, is unfounded in most areas, but certainly among the LMS missionaries in the Northern Cape.

## THE RHENISH MISSIONARY SOCIETY

In the Western Cape, missionaries were working with the slaves and Hottentots in the towns as well as in the mission stations. In Cape Town and some of the nearby villages this work was done by the South African Society. Schools were the main effort, since it was felt that the greatest success was possible with children, and the parents were very concerned that their children learn to read and write, if not become Christians. In 1829, under the aegis of Dr. Philip, the Paris Evangelical Missionary Society and the Rhenish Missionary Society (a German group) sent out missionaries to start new work in South Africa. One of the Paris men accepted a call to work among the slaves at Wellington, and two of the Rhenish men took up work in Stellenbosch and Tulbagh. The other two Rhenish men established the mission stations of Wupperthal near Clanwilliam and Ebenezer at the mouth of the Olifants River. At these stations the missionaries attempted to train the Hottentots who came to them as craftsmen and peasant farmers. Ebenezer was agriculturally hopeless, but being on the main route north to Namaqualand, it was useful as a point of contact. Wupperthal, a farm in the Cedarberg Mountains, became quite successful after a long struggle with the indolent habits of the Hottentots.

In succeeding years the Rhenish Mission opened up new stations in Namaqualand (the area of the Cape Province bounded on the north by the Orange River and on the west by the Atlantic Ocean) and, during the 1840's, took over the remaining LMS stations in that area. In the interior, where Williston and Carnarvon now are, the Rhenish Mission had stations for Coloureds and for Africans (Xhosas who had been placed there by the government). When white farmers moved into these areas, however, the land claims of the missions and their people were overridden by the government in favor of the white farmers. The missionaries moved with some of these people farther north to the present Upington area; but they were again pushed out and they moved northwest into South West Africa.

In the 1930's and 1940's all the stations remaining in the Cape Province were turned over by the Rhenish Mission to the Dutch Reformed Church, except Wupperthal. Some of the members of these churches have resented this switch and have stayed out of the Dutch Reformed Church, but the lack of clergy and the demise of the older generation have brought most people into the Dutch Reformed fold. In many rural areas and small towns, employers pressure the Coloureds to belong to the Dutch Reformed Church. On the basis of marriage statistics, the strengths of the various denominations among Coloureds are as follows: Dutch Reformed (35 percent), Anglican (20 percent), Congregational (12 percent), Roman Catholic (10 percent), Methodist (10 percent), Lutheran (5 percent). A hundred years ago the Congregationalists (LMS) would probably have claimed most of the Coloured Christians, and the Moravians, the Rhenish and Berlin Societies (listed above as Lutherans) would have followed.

## THE WESLEYAN MISSIONARY SOCIETY

The first Methodist meetings in South Africa were organized by British soldiers in Cape Town about 1806. These meetings continued, and about 1812 the soldiers asked the Wesleyan Missionary Society in England to send a minister to Cape Town to serve them and develop the work there. A minister was sent. But when he was refused permission to hold worship services by the Governor, Lord Somerset, he went on to Ceylon. The Rev. Barnabas Shaw was sent to Cape Town in 1816; he did not wait for the governor's permission to preach — he merely did it. His instructions, however, were not to minister to the people of Cape Town but to go out to the heathen.

Just when Shaw was about to seek a site for a mission station, the

Rev. J. H. Schmelen of the LMS in Namaqualand came into Cape Town on a trip to secure supplies. Schmelen convinced him that Namaqualand was a suitable area for his mission. On the journey north, the two men met a Nama chief who told them that he was on his way to Cape Town to try to find a teacher for his people. Shaw took this as a divine call and built his mission station on the Kamiesberg at a place called Leliefontein (or Lily Fountain). Because Leliefontein is near the summit of the mountain, it is one of the few places in the area that gets sufficient rain to grow crops, its altitude even makes it cool enough to grow wheat there, which the missionaries introduced. The people were eager for teaching, though this could take place regularly only during the rainy season, when there was enough pasturage near the mission station. Great progress was made in developing the church and community in the first few decades, even to the extent of the setting up of a hat factory. But in the last half of the nineteenth century, copper mines were opened in Namaqualand and the men went off to work in them, and farther afield to Kimberley and Johannesburg. Thus the mission station became the haven of the elderly and the infirm. Economic and social development not only slowed down, but even regressed in some aspects of life.

The first martyrdom for the missionary cause in South Africa occurred in connection with the Leliefontein mission station. William Threlfall was a young Methodist missionary who arrived in Cape Town in 1822. He was sent first to the Eastern Cape, where he assisted the Rev. William Shaw in organizing congregations among the English settlers. He was eager, however, to pioneer among the heathen, and in 1823 went to Delagoa Bay in order to be nearer Madagascar, where he felt he was really called to serve. In the meantime he sought possibilities for starting a Wesleyan mission at Delagoa Bay. This was to be part of a grand, three-cornered scheme for covering Southern Africa: the Eastern Cape work among the Xhosas was to be one angle, the mission among the Batswana in the north was to be another; and Delagoa Bay was to be the entering point for working west and south to meet the others. In the first few weeks, Threlfall managed to make promising contacts with a tribe living on the Maputa River (not too far from where the Methodist mission in Maputaland, northeastern Natal, now is). But then fever hit him, and he had a very hard time before he got back to Cape Town.

Threlfall spent several months convalescing in Cape Town, then went north to continue his convalescence at Leliefontein. Here he heard about attempts to open mission stations north of the Orange River. Some of the old opponents of Christianity had died or left the area, so there seemed to be some hope for success, though the most formidible enemies of drought and heat (often it was 120 degrees) were still present. Among Barnabas Shaw's converts was a young man named Jacobus Links, who had already gone out to preach in various places to the Bushmen. In July 1826, Threlfall, Jacobus Links and another young Nama, Johannes Jager, set off on an exploratory trip across the Orange River, aiming for the Warmbaths area of what is now South West Africa. But the three were murdered at a Bushman village a few days' journey north of Warmbaths by their Nama guides and the Bushmen, who apparently wanted to plunder their barter goods. In 1834 the Rev. Edward Cook succeeded in establishing permanent Methodist work north of the Orange River, but this was turned over to the Rhenish Mission in 1867.

## THE ANGLICANS AND ROMAN CATHOLICS

Both the Anglican and the Roman Catholic churches now have many coloured members, though neither had any during the first half of the nineteenth century. Congregational polity made it very difficult for the Congregational churches to follow up their members when they left their rural homes to work in the towns and on the mines. Thus, the Congregationalists, as well as the Moravians, tended to remain rural-oriented churches. But the parochial system of the Anglicans and Roman Catholics, and the large staffs they were able to bring into South Africa from overseas enabled these churches to grow in the towns and cities. In recent years the multi-racial character of the Roman Catholic and Anglican churches has made them appealing to many coloureds.

## THE KAT RIVER SETTLEMENT

In the Eastern Cape the largest coloured community was not a mission station but a government-sponsored settlement. This was located on the slopes of the Amatola Mountains and in the valley of the Kat River, a tributary of the Fish in the vicinity of Fort

Beaufort. This area had originally been occupied by Xhosas under the chief Ngqika and was highly desirable because of its relatively high rainfall in the midst of a terrain which suffers from regular droughts. It was, however, in the zone which was supposed to be a buffer, unoccupied, between the colonists and the Xhosas. Therefore, in the late 1820's, the Xhosas were forced to move farther east. Stockenstrom, who was then magistrate at Graaff-Reinet, suggested letting Hottentots and coloureds live there under government sponsorship. He thought they might be able to develop worthwhile communities if they were given suitable allotments of land, and they would also serve as a barrier between the Xhosas and the whites. There was much opposition to the plan because the land was so desirable to white farmers, but the project did get official approval and was started in 1829.

A government-paid minister, the Reverend W. R. Thomson, who had served as a government missionary among the Xhosas since 1822, became minister of the Dutch Reformed Church in the community. Many of the people, however, were church members from Bethelsdorp and Theopolis, both LMS stations, and they wanted an LMS minister. So they called the Rev. James Read from Bethelsdorp and he became their minister. In 1837 James Read, Jr., who had been to England to study and had been tutored in theology by Philip in Cape Town, became school teacher and co-pastor with his father. Another son, Joseph, also became a school teacher.

During the 1830's the reports of the settlement were generally glowing. The people were eager to learn, though, even then, overcrowding was making this difficult. In the wars of 1835 and 1847 the settlement was badly destroyed and the men were all called up for military service, some away from home for several years. When, during the 1840's, the white farmers began hiring African farm laborers, many Hottentots lost their employment and some of these became a drain on the resources of the Kat River people.

In 1851, when yet another frontier war between the Colony and the Xhosas broke out, and the Kat River settlement was again attacked and its men called up for military service, with little likelihood of pay and no way to protect their homes while they were away, some of the men joined with the Xhosas in attacking the colonial troops. The alarm of the white community was great because a general Hottentot uprising might have been the end for the whites, at least in the Eastern Cape. A Grahamstown newspaper was quick to blame the LMS missionaries as fomenters of the rebellion and advocated that all the land at the Kat River be given to white farmers. In the end only a portion of the land was given to whites, but the result was that the character of the place was completely lost and the zeal for improvement which had existed there in previous years died out. Theopolis, where the Hottentots had come to blows with their Fingo neighbors and also attacked the British, ceased to be a mission station. For too many years previously it had had only very old missionaries, and its most progressive people had gone to the Kat River, where they could have freehold land rights (or at least had been promised such). This was a sad denouement to what had once been a thriving mission station.

The mission stations, especially those of the LMS, had other problems during the 1850's. The missionaries themselves were afraid to speak out on public issues — they wanted to live at peace with their white neighbors or perhaps had come to adopt many of their views. They believed firmly, along with most people of the time, that freehold ownership of property was the greatest blessing they could bestow on the inhabitants of the missionary institutions. What they did not foresee was that within a generation most of those freehold farms would have been sold to whites. Without skills and capital to develop their land, the people were not really better off than they had been before. The only asset they had with which to buy the clothing, cooking utensils, and other things the missionaries had helped them feel the need for was their land. To pay their debts, they sold their land. Or, some lost it even more quickly in paying for the brandy which to this day has been the scourge of every coloured community. When whites and coloureds lived side by side, the wealth almost inevitably drained into the white purses, leaving the coloureds as poor as they had ever been, and with greater consciousness of their poverty because of the greater contrast with their neighbors.

Very few coloured ministers were trained during the nineteenth century, though Philip organized a school at Hankey to train teachers and ministers. The LMS had serious financial problems from the middle of the nineteenth century on, and great pressure was exerted from all sides to use what resources it did have to push the work northwards to unevangelized people in the interior. Almost no new missionaries were sent to the coloured churches after about 1860. Those who were already there stayed on, but they were not replaced. Thus the coloured churches came to be sprawling collections of congregations, several thousand members spread over hundreds of square miles sharing a minister — or doing without one for long periods of time — who at best could only administer the sacraments and convene the deacon's court. Revivalist preaching often took the place of teaching, though the Sunday School was sometimes strong, at least in numbers, and Boys' and Girls' Brigades were organized in many congregations. The schools the missionaries had set up to help prepare people for church membership and an informed Christian outlook became the preoccupation of the churches. Nevertheless the churches remained important forces in creating solidarity in the coloured communities.

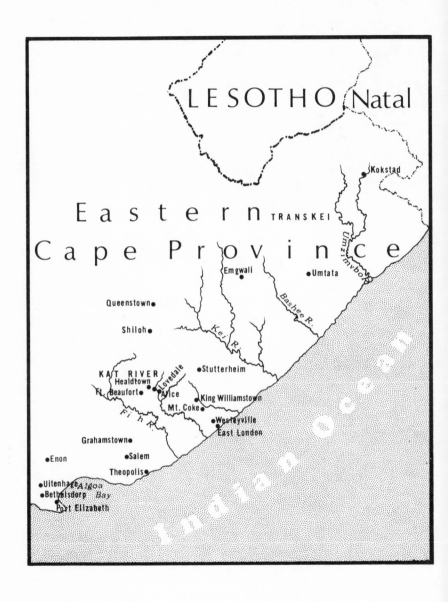

# V

# MISSION WORK AMONG THE XHOSAS

Though he had been chased away, Vanderkemp was not forgotten by the Xhosas. One man who was fascinated by his teaching was a councillor of Chief Ndlambe named Makanda. Makanda made a number of trips to Grahamstown, the military center on the eastern frontier. And each time he spent long hours with the Rev. Mr. Vanderlingen who served as chaplain to the Hottentot soldiers. He asked many questions about guns and war, but even more about theological matters.

> Combining what he had learned respecting the creation, the fall of man, the atonement, the resurrection, and other Christian doctrines, with some of the superstitious traditions of his countrymen and with his own wild fancies, he framed a sort of extravagant religious medley, and, like another Mohammed, boldly announced himself as a prophet and teacher directly inspired from Heaven.[1]

He preached that the tribal ancestors would arise from the dead and assist him and his people to victory in battle. Makanda persuaded Ndlambe and his people to go to war against Ngqika (his nephew for whom he had been regent and to whom he was loath to turn over control of the tribe) in 1818. Ndlambe's people did win, but the next try, against the British at Grahamstown, was not successful. This kind of syncretistic messianism is not, of course, unusual among people who are confronting Western culture for the first time. A similar idea spread among the Xhosas farther east in 1857; they were told that if they slaughtered all their cattle and destroyed all their crops their ancestors and cattle would be resurrected and they would drive all the whites into the sea. Thousands of Xhosas starved to death.

At the time when Makanda was beginning to put forward his new ideas, the London Missionary Society finally received permission from the Governor, Lord Somerset, to send a missionary beyond the boundary of the Colony to open a mission among the Xhosas. The man chosen to do this was Joseph Williams, who made an exploratory trip with James Read in 1816. Later that year Williams and his wife and child went to the site chosen, near the present town of Fort Beaufort on the Kat River. His problems were enormous — language, irrigation (he built a dam across the river and a canal to irrigate his fields), and the suspicion of the paramount Ngqika, whose home was not too far away. His biggest problem, however, lay in the demands made upon him by the government of the Colony. He received messages asking him to look for stolen cattle and turn over thieves. He was expected to send information about what was going on in the tribe to the colonial government. Having given permission to Williams to cross the border, Lord Somerset and Colonel Cuyler, the magistrate at Uitenhage, thought they had a full-time border guard and spy out of the bargain. But Williams felt that to do these government jobs would jeopardize his role as a missionary, so he usually, though not always, refused to do them. For this he was loudly, even publicly, berated. The burden of these things was, perhaps, too much. In any case, after only eighteen months, Williams died. One of the most pathetic accounts in South African mission history is Mrs. Williams' story of how she had to give all the instructions for making a coffin and digging a grave because there was no one with her except the Xhosas and they were totally ignorant of such customs. She wanted to carry on after his death, but the LMS brethren would not permit it.

In spite of its brevity, Williams' work among the Xhosas had significant results. This was largely due to Ntsikana, the convert who kept the followers together until a successor arrived several years later. It is difficult to reconcile the dates of the story of Ntsikana's life as written by J. K. Bokwe with the records of the LMS, but what Bokwe has written is at least the tradition of the Xhosa Christians about Ntsikana.

Ntsikana first heard Vanderkemp when he was a teenager, and

probably heard the Rev. James Read in 1811, when Read preached to the Xhosa on a journey he made. About 1815 Ntsikana had a mystical experience — first a peculiar light which shone on his favorite beast as he viewed the cattle early in the morning (the usual start to the day for a cattle-loving African), and later the same day a weird gale which blew on him alone whenever he danced at a community gathering. He ordered his family to leave the dance early, and on the way home stopped at a river and washed off the red clay which all the Xhosas smeared on their bodies.

The next day Ntsikana began singing a chant which said that Makanda was misleading the people. When asked why he said this and why he was acting so peculiarly, Ntsikana replied, "The thing that has entered within me directs that all should pray; no one understands it in this country as yet, except perhaps Ngcongolo [James Read]." Like many other Xhosas, Ntsikana had sent an ox to Makanda when Makanda announced that he could bring back the ancestors. But after his mystical experience, he sent a messenger to demand back his ox and to denounce Makanda publicly. It was just at this time that Makanda had announced a time and place for the great resurrection: a spot on the beach near where East London now is. Thousands gathered and spent the night on the beach waiting, but nothing happened. Most of Ngqika's people who had flocked to Makanda went back home and some of them began to listen to Ntsikana, but those of Ndlambe continued to follow Makanda in spite of their disappointment.

As Ntsikana continued to oppose Makanda, who began to predict the destruction of the Ngqika people, his following grew and after a time he moved nearer the royal village of Ngqika. He preached there regularly and began praying in people's houses. What he preached is not clear, but most likely the basis of it was what he had learned from Read. Or perhaps this was after Williams arrived and he was learning from Williams. The father of Tiyo Soga, the first ordained minister among the Xhosas, was one of Ntsikana's followers at this time and introduced morning and evening prayers at his own village. He even urged Ngqika to pray (Soga was one of Ngqika's most important councillors). When he was converted Ntsikana had released his second wife and given her some of his property. There is no evidence, however, that he urged others to abandon polygamy. He prophesied the defeat of Ngqika's people by Ndlambe's at Amalinde and also the arrival of the Fingo people, refugees from Tshaka who began to push in among the Xhosas in the early 1820's.

In 1820 the Rev. John Brownlee began to build a mission station in the Tyume (Chumie) valley, and Ntsikana thought of moving there with his people. He became ill. Realizing that his illness would be fatal, he urged his followers to go to the Tyume mission after his death, which some of them did. He wanted to be buried in a coffin, doubtless remembering Mrs. Williams' preparations for her husband's burial. Having no planks, he ordered that a tree trunk be hollowed out. A funeral service was conducted by two followers who were already in contact with Brownlee, Noyi (known after his baptism as Robert Balfour) and Matshaya (Charles Henry).

Another of Williams' helpers, whom one meets throughout the early history of missions in the Eastern Cape, was Jan Tshatshu (spelled in myriad ways). Tshatshu was the son of the chief of the Amantinde tribe, who lived where King William's Town is now. The chief visited Vanderkemp at Bethelsdorp and left his son there to go to school. Jan Tshatshu accompanied Read and Williams on their exploratory tour, translated for them, and preached and prayed in Xhosa on his own. The people responded enthusiastically to his preaching, the first ever done directly in Xhosa. When they returned to Bethelsdorp, before leaving for their permanent occupation at the Kat River, Tshatshu married a Hottentot woman and she accompanied him. They stayed with Williams for more than a year, leaving about four months before Williams died. Tshatshu went to Theopolis, where he assisted Mr. Barker, a missionary there.

After Williams' death, the Rev. John Brownlee, an LMS missionary who had severed his connection with the LMS and accepted a post as government missionary to Ngqika's people, enlisted Tshatshu to accompany him. Since the Xhosas had been evicted from the Kat River valley, they settled in the valley of the Tyume River, a few miles north of where the village of Alice is now. In 1825 Brownlee returned to service with the LMS and founded a new mission station at Tshatshu's original home on the Buffalo River (now King William's Town). In 1836 Dr. Philip took Tshatshu, who was chief himself by then, to Britain along with a Hottentot Christian. They were lionized by the mission audiences and given much attention by the Aborigines' Protection Society. Many colonists claimed, a decade later, that Tshatshu had been spoiled by all the attention he received in England and that this was the cause of his not supporting the

British in the wars of 1847 and 1850-51. He continued as a lay preacher in the church until his old age. At the time of his death the place where he lived had passed through the stages of being a tribal village, a mission station, a British military camp, and the capital of the colony of British Kaffraria. By that time King William's Town was the center of trade for Kaffraria (the Ciskei — the area between the Fish and Kei Rivers) and the Transkei (the area between the Kei River and the Natal border).

The Glasgow Missionary Society had long been in consultation with the London Missionary Society, and in the early 1820's it had two candidates ready to send to the Eastern Cape to work among the Xhosas (Kaffirs, or Caffres, as they were then called). Permission from the Cape government was the obstacle, but it happened that just at that time Lord Somerset determined that an assistant for Mr. Brownlee was needed. Thus the Rev. W. R. Thomson was appointed a government missionary like Brownlee, and he was accompanied by Mr. John Bennie, whose salary was paid by the Glasgow Missionary Society. Thomson and Bennie went to live at Tyume with Brownlee and his family. When several more Glasgow missionaries arrived a couple of years later, new mission stations were founded a few miles away. By 1830 there were four or five stations within twenty miles of each other. Mr. Bennie, later ordained, became a well-known Xhosa scholar, and when the Rev. John Ross brought a printing press with him, a beginning was made at the publication of scripture portions and school materials in Xhosa. In later years the printing establishment was moved to Lovedale, and Lovedale remains the foremost source of Xhosa literature, though the first complete Bible in Xhosa was published by the Methodists at Mount Coke in 1859.

To understand what the Cape government expected of its government missionaries, it is interesting to look at the instructions issued to Thomson and Brownlee at the time of Brownlee's appointment:

> There is, perhaps, no circumstance connected with the interests of his Majesty's government in this settlement, that his excellency Lord C. H. Somerset feels more anxiously alive to, than the introduction of Christianity among our enlightened neighbours, and with it, its invariable concomitant, and greatest of temporal blessings to a people, "civilization."

> Independent of the duty which his excellency feels to be imposed upon him, to give every aid in his power to the

diffusion of the principles of our holy religion, thereby to be the humble means of recovering some few from the deplorable darkness in which they are lamentably still plunged; independent of the gratification a liberal and feeling mind must experience, from having it in his power to aid in spreading the arts of civilized society among hordes still in a state of the grossest barbarism; his excellency is convinced, that he shall better consult the immediate interests of the settlements committed to his charge, and put more easily a stop to those inhuman massacres and ruinous plunderings, which take place on our border, by complying with the wish of the Caffre chief, to have a zealous and enlightened instructor sent to him, than by any acts of hostility against the offending Caffres.

His excellency, aware that you have been educated with the view to your carrying religious instruction to the heathen, begs to say, that it is not in any shape his intention to prescribe any particular method for you to adopt on this head. . . . But his excellency will be desirous of regular and correct information of the progress made by the Caffre people in the principles we profess, and of the numbers who embrace the Christian faith.

His excellency's chief object, next to this of religious instruction, is, that you should constantly impress upon the chiefs, his friendly feelings in this regard; that you should explain to them his wish, that the border now fixed should not be violated by either; that, on his part, he is prepared to punish any colonist who shall commit the most trifling offence against the Caffre people; and that it is but just, in return, that the Caffre chiefs should, on their parts, seek out and punish those who commit depredations and murders in our territory. His excellency is anxious to establish such an intercourse between the Caffre people and the colonists as shall be mutually beneficial; and for this end, he is desirous of obtaining correct statements as to their wants, and also as to the objects they may bring to Graham's Town for barter. . . .

Nothing can be more clear than the immorality of the Caffre aggression on the colony; nothing more distinct than the peaceable and friendly views of the colonial government towards the Caffres. It requires, therefore, that they should be convinced of their injustice, and that they should see the impolicy of their proceedings. If they live at peace with the colony, their own welfare may be secured by it, and their wants supplied; a contrary system brings upon them those evils which have visited their people ever since it became necessary to expel them from our territory.[2]

Mr. Thomson took these instructions seriously, and within a few years his relations with Ngqika and all his councillors were so strained that he could do no useful mission work and his health broke down. In 1829 he took the position of Dutch Reformed Church pastor to the Hottentots and coloureds at the Kat River settlement. Brownlee concentrated on what he considered mission work and refused to do what the government wanted him to do. Even before Thomson resigned, Brownlee had left Tyume and quit his government post. He found that serving the LMS gave him much more freedom to work as he thought fit.

An interesting question about the early Xhosa missions is to what extent their early followers were Xhosas. By 1830 each of the mission stations had several hundred people living around them. Sometimes these were people who had gotten in trouble with a chief or had been accused of witchcraft. But many of them, it seems, were Gonaqua Hottentots, or people of mixed Hottentot and Xhosa ancestry. The area where the first mission stations were founded is an area where Hottentots and Xhosas had been mixing for about two hundred years. But it would appear that some of these people were not thoroughly integrated into the tribal life. In a sense they were already detribalized, and so the mission station offered a security they did not feel in the Xhosa villages. Others may from time to time have worked in the Colony and developed an interest in education and a desire for some of the ways of the white man. The evidence for this kind of thing is very meager, but it is an interesting question because it pertains to the matter of what impact the missions had on their environment and what response there was to the missionary's message. The eager listening of thousands to Read's and Tshatshu's message did not continue. Interest changed to hostility, probably because of the overall condemnation of Xhosa customs by the missionaries. The relations of the Xhosas with the Colony did not make the job easy either. Cattle thefts and retaliatory raids were common occurrences. And political instability among the Xhosa chiefs was probably another factor making the missionaries' task more difficult; they were pawns in the struggle, sometimes.

In 1823 the Rev. William Shaw, who had gone to South Africa as the pastor of a party of Wesleyan settlers in 1820, set up the first Methodist station for the Xhosas. The site was called Wesleyville, located between the Keiskhama and Buffalo Rivers, about ten miles inland from the ocean. Shaw had had very great success in organizing circuits for Europeans in the Eastern Cape who were almost without clergy. His aim was that the white congregations provide the personnel and money for missionary enterprises among the Africans. This goal was very largely accomplished. Many Methodist missionaries were themselves 1820 settlers or the sons of 1820 settlers, members of Shaw's congregation at Salem or somewhere else in the circuit. These men and their wives comprised the bulk of the missionaries who served the chain of mission stations which Shaw organized from Grahamstown to Natal and also the half dozen or so Methodist missions in what is now the Orange Free State. They had far fewer problems of adjustment than those who came from London or Glasgow to serve as missionaries. Most of them started as catechists and were ordained only after they had served several years on a mission station, doing manual labor and teaching in the schools, as well as preaching and studying for the ministry. Shaw's careful superintendence made this kind of system workable.

There was, however, criticism of the Methodist system of moving missionaries at short intervals; it was difficult for the missionaries to become proficient in the language and to build up the confidence of the local people. Whereas Brownlee lived with the same tribe for nearly fifty years, a Methodist missionary might have worked with as many as six different language groups during his ministry.

By 1830, Shaw was able to report considerable progress at Wesleyville:

> ... religious ordinances were regularly maintained; the number of inquirers and converts steadily increased. The sabbath was fully recognized by the people at Wesleyville and in all the surrounding neighbourhood. The school was in active operation. The plough had been introduced. A store, under the care of Mr. R. Walker, was established for supplying clothing and useful articles to the natives, in return for the raw produce of the country.[3]

When Shaw went exploring to find a site for his first mission station, he went first to Tyume and conferred with Thomson and Brownlee. They helped him set up at Wesleyville, and it was agreed that the Methodists would confine their efforts to the tribes along the coast while the Glasgow Society would serve Ngqika's people. This arrangement was generally satisfactory until after the war of 1835, when the government moved tribes from one area to another. This happened again after the wars of 1847 and 1850-51. The end result was that Methodists and Presbyterians (Glasgow Missionary Society) were thoroughly intermingled throughout the Ciskei and Transkei.

Both groups had more success at first with the Fingo peoples — those Zulus who had been pushed south by Tshaka's wars. They were living as serfs among the Xhosas. Already a detribalized and subject people, perhaps it is natural that they would be more attracted to the mission stations and the prospects of education. During the wars they allied themselves with the British and fought against the Xhosas. And at the end of each war they got the good land that Xhosas were deprived of as punishment for having gone to war against the British. Thus there was little love between the Fingoes and the Xhosas, and this feeling tended to increase throughout the nineteenth century. A church with both Fingo and Xhosa members was impossible. The Methodist Church became the church of many Fingoes and also of the Pondos, a tribe who lived much nearer the Natal border. The chiefs of the Xhosas tended to feel that by befriending the Fingoes the Methodists had betrayed them. Some Methodists also publicly took the part of the British settlers (to whom many of them were pastors) in the argument over whose fault the war of 1835 was, whereas some of the Presbyterians and LMS missionaries blamed the colonists and the British government for having taken away the land of the Xhosas. This argument was a cause of tension between these two groups of missionaries for many years, and doubtless hampered what interdenominational cooperation there might have been.

Education became the biggest business of the missionaries. As early as the 1820's the Glasgow missionaries, meeting as the Presbytery of Caffraria, expressed the need for a boarding school where youths could be taken away from the heathen atmosphere of their homes (apparently even the missionary stations were tainted because what they first wanted was some place in the Colony) and trained as teachers and pastors. It was not until 1841, however, that Lovedale Missionary Institute, the first boarding school, was founded. The unique thing about Lovedale was that it was a school for both Africans and whites. The whites were primarily the children of missionaries, but also the sons of farmers and others in the vicinity. The Africans were chosen by examination from those who had completed the work available at village schools. Until it was taken over by the Bantu Education Department in 1954, Lovedale remained the most prestigious African school in the Republic. For years it was the highest level school for Africans, and then it spawned Fort Hare University College, the first degree-level institution for non-whites in South Africa (1916).

Other missions organized boarding schools in the nineteenth century. Government grants were first available under Governor Sir George Grey in the 1850's, whose policy on the frontier was that money should be spent on schools and hospitals for the Xhosas instead of on armies. Grey was the first civilian governor at the Cape after the British occupation. The Methodists built a school at Healdtown (hear Fort Beaufort) where teachers and ministers were trained. The first boarding school for African girls was founded in 1861 at Emgwali by the Presbyterians.

The Moravians and the Berlin Mission had mission stations north and east of the Tyume mission. Shiloh, the Moravian station, was organized as a communal farm with its own milling and store facilities; for a number of years it showed a profit. The Berlin Mission was near Stutterheim; but this was in an area where whites were later given land, and its work became difficult on that account. The Moravians eventually opened other mission stations in the Transkei, but the Berlin Mission continued to have only the one.

When Bishop Gray of the Anglican Church arrived in 1848, he set off to visit all of South Africa with a view to ascertaining its church needs. As a result of this, and later visitations, and the work of Archdeacon Merriman of Grahamstown, the Anglicans started mission work among the Xhosas at Grahamstown, near King William's Town, near Queenstown, and at Umtata. In parts of the Transkei the work was undertaken by an order within the Anglican Church (the Society of St. John the Evangelist). Industrial training and other types of schools were an important part of their mission work, as were hospitals.

Though a few Africans were involved as soon as there were Roman Catholic clergy in the Eastern Cape, large-scale mission work by the Roman Catholics did not begin among the Xhosas until the 1880's. They, too, established comprehensive mission stations, with a variety of schools and medical facilities, as well as churches. Extensive agricultural training was undertaken at some mission stations.

The frontier wars were over when the Anglican and Roman Catholic missions were founded. The Xhosa people were a conquered people. Many, of course, still clung to the ways of their fathers, but the power of the chiefs was broken, and, for many, the way out seemed to be to adopt the ways of their conquerors. The mission stations offered an initiation into the white man's ways. School attendance meant church attendance, and, sometimes, baptism and church membership. The successful ones became school teachers, and church membership was usually required for such jobs. This is not to say that there were not sincere Christians – there were many – but that there were also many whose convictions were not deep enough to have caused them to become Christians in the earlier days when it meant a much sharper break with family and village. And soon, of course, there came to be children who had grown up on the mission stations, second and third generation Christians. Some of these were a great disappointment to the missionaries, who had hoped that they might know nothing and care nothing for the ways of the heathen only to discover that this was not the case. Others, however, became faithful teachers and ministers, some even going as missionaries to central Africa.

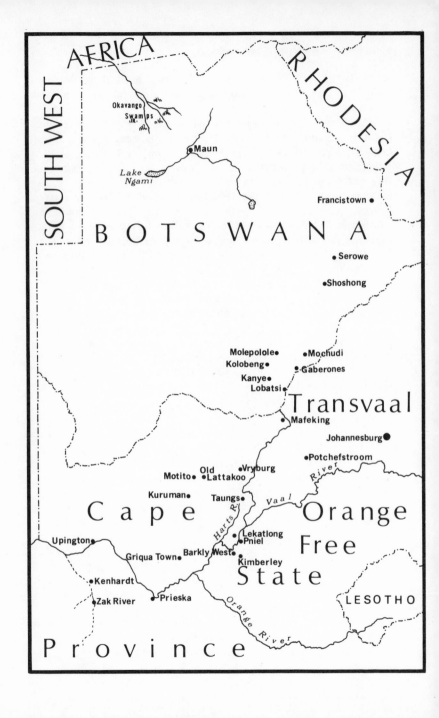

# VI

# THE NORTHERN CAPE AND BOTSWANA

When the Rev. John Campbell toured Southern Africa on behalf of the London Missionary Society in 1812 and 1813, he went north from Griqua Town to visit the Batswana people, about whom he had heard from the Griquas and white hunters. Campbell's description of the Batlapin Batswana is one of the earliest. From the Batlapin chief, he got permission for a missionary to live in the town of Lattakoo. The chief agreed to this because he wanted trade with the Colony, especially for guns and ammunition. The early missionaries, including the Rev. James Read, who served there for a time, along with Hottentot helpers from Bethelsdorp and Griqua helpers from Griqua Town, had a difficult time because of these expectations. In fact, to remain there and to have an audience for their preaching, they were forced to give presents and carry on trade. The Rev. Robert Moffat, who had already had some experience with nomadic peoples in Great Namaqualand (southern South West Africa), refused to continue this expensive tradition, but his real success among the Batswana began only after they were considerably dislocated by raids from marauding groups pushed out by the Zulus. In fact, only when Moffat established his own site, where he himself was chief, did he succeed in establishing a Christian community. This was at Kuruman, some distance from the chief.

After Moffat, the second great missionary to the Batswana was David Livingstone, who served for a time at Kuruman, but became restless to move into the unexplored regions to the north. He established several mission stations in what is now Botswana and one in what is now the western Transvaal. He did not get along with his Boer neighbors. He accused them (publicly in print) of dealing in slaves, and they accused him of selling ammunition to the Batswana. The end of the argument was that the Boers sacked Livingstone's home at Kolobeng. Two LMS missionaries, Inglis and Edwards, were driven out of the Transvaal because of similar charges on both sides. Livingstone explored to the north and west in Botswana, and even farther north into what is now Zambia. He publicized these areas and the fact that there were no missionaries to serve them. Unfortunately, the broad sheet of water he discovered (Lake Ngami) was a dried-up par with swamps at one end by the time more missionaries arrived there a few years later. It was not until the twentieth century that permanent mission work in Ngamiland, centered at the village of Maun, was undertaken. There are still areas in the northwest of Botswana where churches, schools, and hospitals are virtually unknown. This is true of most of western Botswana, but only the north has sufficient water to provide sustenance to any but tiny groups of wandering Bushmen.

As early as 1805 some of the missionaries to the peoples north of the Orange River had had some contact with the Batswana (Batlapin). There had been no conversions, or even any interest in Christianity, but it was reported that a new method of plowing had been introduced. When Campbell visited the area in 1813 he conceived the idea of putting a missionary at work immediately at translating the Bible into Setswana, a language which, he had been told, was understood by many other tribes to the north and east. His idea was that as each book of the Bible was translated, it should be copied and sent out to the various tribes by runners who could read. Campbell thought it should be possible for a missionary to learn the language and begin translating within six months. Thus, the whole of the Setswana tribes could be evangelized in a very few years!

But when Moffat undertook to learn Setswana (he was the first to do so — his predecessors had preached in Dutch and had Hottentots translate for them), he worked at it for nearly five years before beginning to translate. And that translation became his lifework. William Ashton, who joined Moffat at Kuruman in 1843, worked at his side for the last seven of the thirty years Moffat spent translating the scriptures. Revision of his work began before Moffat died and continues to the present. Whether Moffat's work was helped or hindered by his attitude toward the Batswana — he thought they had no religious ideas at all, or at least none worth bothering about — is questionable. He also felt that all their customs were wicked; the only proper response to them was denunciation. While Moffat labored over the language and the creation of a well-watered oasis in the midst of a parched land, his wife devoted her energies to covering the nakedness of her neighbors. On his speaking tours in Britain, Moffat did not hesitate to point out how well the textile manufacturing towns of England had profited from the work of the missionaries. With David Livingstone, his son-in-law, Moffat shared the idea that Christianity and commerce should go hand in hand.

Because he saw his aims clearly and pushed hard to achieve them, Moffat was undoubtedly the leader of the LMS Batswana Mission, but he wanted to be left alone to do his own work the way he saw fit, and he assumed that others preferred to work in the same way. During the 1840's a District Committee was set up to direct policy for the LMS in the area. But Moffat could not be bothered with such, and so from 1849 to 1866 it did not meet. This was a source of frustration to other missionaries who wanted fellowship and support in their work.

Moffat's idea of the church was of a small group of morally purified and fully committed Christians. There were never more than a hundred members at Kuruman in Moffat's time, and there were many cases of excommunication. Hope was placed in those who grew up on the mission station and had been to school, but even these were often disappointing. Some who it was thought would serve the church as preachers and teachers took well-paying jobs in the growing towns.

In 1849 and 1850 the Rev. J. J. Freeman made a visit to all of the LMS mission stations in Southern Africa. When he visited Kuruman, he saw the need for theological students but saw also that it would be impossible to find young men to give themselves for training. They were already married and deeply involved in pastoral and agricultural responsibilities for their families. Two other possibilities suggested themselves. One was to take children out of their home environment and bring them up in the missionary family:

> They must be secluded not only from the heathen portion of the community, but from their home, habits, customs, and occupations, even though the parents may be Christians, lest

they imbibe that love of a life among flocks and herds, by
which natives seem animated.[1]

The other suggestion was that for the time being older men might,
with some special training, be able to provide the leadership needed.
These should be men whose piety and morality had already been
tested.

In visiting the various stations, Freeman concluded that some of
them were a dead end as far as extension of the mission was
concerned. In several, the missionary had worked for years without
apparent response. Others, however, including Livingstone's station
at Koboleng (in spite of the nakedness of the people, and their
grease and red ochre) offered some hope. At Lekatlong (Likhatlong),
where Mr. Helmore was missionary, Freeman found, out of a
population of 1,200, a church congregation of 600, with 300
communicants. The absence of the children from the mission station
because of their work at the cattle posts, was, however, a
disadvantage.

In the second half of the nineteenth century, land ownership
created problems in some mission stations, especially in Kuruman
and Taungs. The Rev. J. S. Moffat, who succeeded his father for a
time at Kuruman, wrote in 1870: "It would be a blessing if the land
incumbrances of this station could be got rid of. . . . The landlord
relation to the people interferes with our spiritual power, apart from
the distraction of thought, and waste of time."[2] In the second half
of the twentieth century this problem has been more or less dealt
with, not by the transfer of land ownership to someone else, but by
the government policy of Group Areas, causing the Batswana people
to move elsewhere.

Urban mission work began about 1870, when Mr. Ashton
suddenly found his mission station at Barkly West to be in the midst
of the diamond miners. Christians and non-Christians of many
languages gathered to work. In spite of the wickedness of much that
went on at the diamond diggings, there was an eager response to
mission work. Bibles and hymnbooks were especially sought after,
and offerings at services generously contributed to.

At the time of the last frontier war in the Eastern Cape,
disaffected Xhosas travelled through Griqualand West and British
Bechuanaland (the Kuruman part of the Northern Cape), spreading
rumors and inviting people to kill the whites and take over their
houses. A trader and his family were killed at Daniel's Kuil by their

Batswana servants. The Europeans throughout the area, including all the missionaries, gathered at Kuruman for protection, and no harm came to any, though the station at Motito was destroyed. The British government sent the Warren Expedition to insure peace in the area. The Rev. John Mackenzie, an LMS missionary who had worked for some years in Botswana, accompanied Warren.

For three years there was a British police force in the area, but then it was withdrawn. After its withdrawal, the number of filibusters and freebooters increased rapidly. The "republics" of Goshen and Stellaland were proclaimed, where Vryburg and Mafeking now are. Mackenzie went on furlough and argued strongly about the need in Botswana for protection from the Boers and the adventurers. At about the same time, German interest in South West Africa became apparent. And in February 1884 a convention was signed announcing a British Protectorate over all the country not included in the Transvaal. Mackenzie was appointed Deputy Commissioner for Bechuanaland, but he was replaced soon after because, it was stated, of his tactless dealings with the Boers. Cecil Rhodes, however, had been maneuvering to be appointed in his place.

The next two decades of Botswana history were what happened when both the LMS missionaries and Cecil Rhodes tried to get the British Colonial Office to do what they thought best. The best part for the LMS missionaries was the visit of several of the Batswana chiefs to Britain in 1895. The missionary Willoughby supervised their activities, and they were given an excellent press, as well as crowds to hear them speak. The British public was roused to sympathy. The most dramatic incident involving Cecil Rhodes was the Jameson Raid in the next year. As a result of this *faux pas,* Rhodes lost the chance to swallow up the territory of the Batswana chiefs, as he had swallowed up territory in Rhodesia. The southern territories of the Batswana were incorporated into the Cape Colony (in the days before Rhodes had worked out the plans for his own personal empire). The northern areas constitute what is now the independent nation of Botswana. The missionaries may be said to have preserved its identity for eventual independence, but they have never had the wherewithal to bring it economically into the modern world. By and large, the people of Botswana are still living the largely pastoral life they have always known, in addition to working as migrants in the mines of the Republic of South Africa. Botswana's own mineral resources are still untapped and industrial development has not yet begun.

After his wide-ranging trips to the east and west coasts of Africa, into Angola and through the valley of the Zambesi, Livingstone became impatient to open up work among the more heavily populated areas farther north. He convinced the Directors of the London Missionary Society in 1857 that two new missions should be established simultaneously, both using Kuruman as a springboard into the interior: one of these was to the Makololo, living in the swampy headwaters of the Zambesi, the other to the Matabele in the area of Bulawayo. The first of these efforts was a great tragedy, involving the death of Rev. and Mrs. Holloway Helmore, two of the four children who went with them, Mrs. Rogers Price, and the Prices' child. Only the Rev. Roger Price and two Helmore children survived. The cause of the deaths was probably malaria, but poisoning was also suspected. The missionaries had been led to expect that Livingstone himself would meet them on the Zambesi and help them establish the mission. Apparently Livingstone felt he had made no such commitment. Price, and the Mackenzies, who were supposed to join the others (but actually found Price and the Helmore children struggling to return to Kuruman), became missionaries to the Batswana, helping to constitute a chain of missions between Kuruman and the Matabele (Ndebele) mission, which had managed to survive, though its early prospects looked grim.

The Batswana consist of a number of tribal groups, mainly stretched along the eastern margin of Botswana and the western Transvaal, and the northern Cape. Moffat and his colleagues early made contact with the Batlapin and the Bataung in the northern Cape. The Methodist missionaries have served the Barolong people since the early 1820's and helped them move into the Thaba Nchu area of the Orange Free State. By the 1850's, an African teacher went to live among the Bangwaketse, but a missionary (LMS) was sent there only in 1870; the mission station at Kanye is the center of this work. Also in the 1850's Chief Sechele, under David Livingstone, opened the work among the Bakwena. During the next decade Dutch Reformed missionaries in the Transvaal made contact with the Bakgatla people, which eventually led to the development of their mission station at Mochudi in Botswana. The Bamangwato, whose Chief Kgama (Khama) is one of the great heroes of missionary literature, also received their first missionaries during the 1860's, though earlier both Moffat and Livingstone had passed through

Bamangwato country, and Moffat had even been embroiled in Bamangwato politics, having negotiated the release of the heir to the throne from Ndebele (Matabele) captivity. The Batawana people of the Lake Ngami district had no permanent mission work until much later.

Both Chief Sechele and Chief Kgama lived long and had long associations with missionaries. Sechele acted independently after Livingstone had left him, and secured his own missionaries, those of the Hermannsburg Society, acquired for him by Boers of the Transvaal. He later became convinced that such a close relationship with the Boers was not desirable, and the Lutheran missionaries departed. For many years, Roger Price was missionary to Sechele and his people. The two men had a great deal of respect for each other, but there was also much tension between them. Sechele felt that the church should be a tribal institution, over which he should have supervision, as he did over all other tribal business. Price thought otherwise. Though Price had his difficulties, he had real opportunities for preaching and teaching and for influencing the affairs of the tribe as they were discussed in the *kgatla*, the tribal council. Sechele refused to give up his part in the rain-making ceremonies and the initiation rites for the boys. Because of these things he was refused the sacrament of the Lord's Supper, though he had much earlier put away all but one of his wives and had been admitted to church membership. Sechele hoped that Christianity might be grafted upon the heathen customs of the tribe, but the LMS missionaries were very much afraid that a syncretistic church would soon be no church at all. The gate to church membership and church leadership did not open easily; those who got in had strength and a firm understanding of the Christian faith.

Among the Bamangwato the introduction of Christianity coincided with fighting between various contenders for the chieftainship. The acceptance of Christianity by Kgama and Kgamane, two of the sons of the reigning chief (or regent, according to his enemies), contributed to the hostilities, for many in the tribe feared that the safety of the tribe might be jeopardized by a Christian chief who would not follow the customary ways. During the early years Mackenzie and Price were both stationed among the Bamangwato. Times were so difficult that their mere survival in the place was a cause for rejoicing. The most critical time for the missionaries was the period when all five of the old chief's sons refused to be circumcised and take part in the initiation rites. This led to fighting between various sections of the tribe. When Kgama became chief he had always to act cautiously in introducing measures which brought change, especially the kind of changes the missionaries desired, for the possibility of the tribe's splitting always existed.

Kgama's greatest aim as a Christian chief was to enforce prohibition in his territory. This was not a simple matter because the traders with their brandy wagons were always ready to come in and make a profit off of the weakness of his people. He favored education, but was unwilling to push his people faster than they were willing to go on this matter. The attempt of the LMS to build an industrial and high school at Serowe did not receive his backing. In 1905, a man who surveyed educational work in Botswana on behalf of the British government wrote this:

> Chief Khama [Kgama] .... embodies a warning to all reformers in native affairs who attempt too sudden a transition from native ways of life to the ways of Europeans. He shows us that the man who seeks to lead his tribe more than a very few steps toward our civilization must himself, whether a chief or not, be content to wait for the slow operation of education and experience among his people.[3]

Mackenzie recognized the slow pace of change, but he was sanguine that the changes which began to take place were good ones, even though they were far from all he wanted. Sunday observance came to be accepted by the people within a few years of his arrival. He wrote:

> At present they show outward respect to Sunday for much the same reason as they perform any of their old religious services – from fear of the consequences of the opposite course. .... But every act of reverence to the new religion is an act of treason to the old customs. As the power of the one increases in the minds of the people the influence of the other will lose its hold.[4]

Mackenzie saw the appeal of segregated Christian villages of the type that arose in many other parts of Africa, but he felt that the influence of the missionary was greater when he lived in the community where both heathen as well as Christian could observe his way of life and the relations among members of his family. His wife could help all in the community with medicines and sewing. Though the mission houses were sometimes a little way from the village in order to have room for the mission garden and school, as well as the church, there have never been separated Christian villages in Botswana.

Shoshong, Mackenzie's station, was a city of about 30,000 people in the 1860's. He felt the need of a large church; European traders gave money for it, Africans contributed cattle and ostrich feathers which were sold for funds, and the chief commandeered men to fetch wood and grass for the building; the LMS paid only a small part of the cost. The opening of the church was a great occasion, to which all of the people came. First there was a meeting at the church, at which all the contributors were thanked and the building was dedicated, and then there was a feast at the mission house. Some were reluctant to enter the church, thinking the whole thing a trap whereby the Christians who had been persecuted earlier would retaliate on their persecutors. The men arrived arrayed in all varieties of dress and undress. The comments on the building were instructive of the minds of those who entered: "What a splendid place to drink beer in!" "What a capital pen for sheep and goats!"; others declared that it would make a useful fort against the Ndebele. As a result of the interest generated by this event, Mackenzie was able to visit and teach groups of men and even women in the courtyards of all the headmen of the city.[5] The outline of the teaching which Mackenzie gave at these courtyard sessions was this: Creation, Fall, Life, Death and Resurrection of Jesus, Judgment, Ten Commandments, Jesus' teaching about the Ten Commandments, Damnation, God's Love and Forgiveness, the Holy Spirit. It ended with an invitation to those present to accept Jesus as Savior. In the catechumen class, Mackenzie used the Westminster Shorter Catechism as the basis of his teaching.

Mackenzie felt that it was possible to have too many missionaries. There were usually stronger Christians in the outstations, he found, than on the mission stations, because at the latter people tended to take the missionary's word for everything, whereas at the outstations the church people had to read the Bible themselves and work out their own answers. The Bechuana (Batswana) Mission was, in his estimate, weak on training African leaders. He was also aware of the very great influence exerted by the first missionary in a particular place:

> Their type of piety, their mode of thought, and administra-
> tion, will be copied by their disciples. So long as the original

Christian spirit is present in the copy there is nothing to reprehend. But the slavish following out of the letter when the spirit has fled would seem to explain many of the abuses which have been perpetuated in the Christian Church.[6]

The three customs about which the missionaries were most critical were rain-making, initiation, and *bogadi* (cattle payments for wives — what is called *lobola* in Zulu). But by the time there were many people in the churches, the churches themselves prayed for rain and whatever else happened did not trouble the church leaders very much. At Shoshong, Price made an effort to have the chief adopt a modified type of initiation rite, but this was not acceptable. In time, this became the crucial matter — a young man's sincerity as a Christian was tested by his refusal to participate in the initiation rites. For quite a long time, *bogadi* did not seem to be an important issue. But the second generation of Botswana missionaries, led by the Rev. Charles Williams and the Rev. A. J. Wookey, pushed the District Committee in 1875 to pass the following rule:

> That *bogadi* being an evil we endeavour to discourage it by the following means: (a) by refusing to marry unless a promise is given that there is no *bogadi*; (b) by circulating a printed statement that the missionaries are entirely against it; and (c) Church members who countenance *bogadi* either in giving it or receiving it are to be regarded as under church discipline.

Probably the second-generation Batswana Christians, as well as the second-generation missionaries, felt a need for this kind of a law. All wanted the answers given to them by the missionaries, instead of working them out in Bible study, as the early outstation people did.

The Dutch Reformed Mission among the Bakgatla people, with its center at Mochudi, serves a fairly limited area and is well organized in that area. In 1892 the chief, Lentswe, became a church member. He abolished the initiation rites and *bogadi* in his tribe. The Dutch Reformed Mission was the only one permitted in his territory (this was true also for the LMS in the Bamangwato area). By 1908 there was in each village a well-organized school system based on the Sechuana schools. Each school was built by the village and staffed by an unpaid Mutswana. At Mochudi there was a middle school, taught by a Dutch lady with Batswana assistants, and a higher school taught in English. This was, apparently, the best-run school system in Botswana at the time. Lentswe's abolition of *bogadi* was reinforced by a rinderpest epidemic in 1896; but when the herds began to flourish again early in the twentieth century, people began secretly to resume the practice. By 1920 all the non-Christians were engaging openly in it, and many Christians were quietly turning over *bogadi* cattle. In 1927 the Church agreed that *bogadi* was not in itself bad, and the injunction against it was lifted. Theoretically, it was acknowleged, the man's family is free to decide how many cattle they will give to the girl's family; these are publicly displayed as an announcement of the intended marriage. The church authorities discovered, when they changed the rule, that more evils had been caused by prohibiting *bogadi* than by permitting it. To this day, in spite of the central role which church affairs play in the lives of many Bakgatla, magic and sorcery are very real for most people. This is probably true not only of members of the Dutch Reformed Church, but of members of the other churches of Botswana as well.

In the early 1920's the Seventh Day Adventists started medical work at Kanye among the Bangwaketse people. And much more recently the Anglicans have developed work, moving south from the Diocese of Matabeleland and west from Zeerust in the western Transvaal. At Gaberones, the new capital since independence, there is a united Anglican and Congregational church.

The Subia are a minor tribe living near the Chobe River in the far north of Botswana; they have usually been subordinate to the Barotse or Bamangwato or some other more powerful tribe. In 1931 a white evangelist named Maree walked from Francistown to Kachikau on the Chobe River. Maree called his sect the Latter Rain Assemblies of South Africa. After making a number of converts in the Kachikau area, Maree set off for Francistown again, but was killed by Bushmen on the way. His followers split over leadership after some time, but this breach was healed in 1948. Presumably the church is still going on.

In each tribal area there are one or more separatist groups, but they are not nearly as strong as such groups within the Republic of South Africa. Most such organizations have arisen in connection with some dissension over tribal leadership, a sect group being an effective way for a minority to continue to meet and propagate its views.

Roman Catholics were not permitted to do any mission work in Botswana until fairly recently. They have in the country one boarding high school, near Gaberone, and a few priests.

The country as a whole is still trying desperately to get sufficient high schools and industrial training schools (one agricultural training school is about all there is). Botswana cooperates in the University of Lesotho, Botswana, and Swaziland, which is located at Roma in Lesotho. But there are few students from Botswana. Therefore whatever help missions can offer in the way of teachers and schools is desperately wanted by Botswana. This is also true of medical work. Northwestern Botswana is probably one of the few places in Africa where real pioneering work can still be found. The main missionary task at the present seems to be training and guidance for leaders in all areas of the church's life.

# VII

# THE ORANGE FREE STATE

In the early 1820's the Wesleyan Missionary Society sent the Rev.
and Mrs. Samuel Broadbent, who had served briefly at Leliefontein,
across the barren lands known as Bushmanland to Griqua Town with
the intention of starting a new mission in the interior. On the way,
however, Broadbent was seriously injured in an accident and he went
on from Griqua Town to Graaff-Reinet instead of moving north or
east into the interior. After a number of months in Graaff-Reinet
Broadbent, with new colleagues, the Rev. and Mrs. Thomas
Hodgson, returned to the Griqua country. They made contact with
the Koranna people who lived in what is now the Orange Free State
and travelled with them for some time. Broadbent and Hodgson
wanted to work among the Batswana people. They heard from
various sources about the Barolong people, Sifonelo's people, and
wanted to investigate the possibilities of a mission to them. The
Korannas, however, made this project very difficult, whether from
reasons of fear or of greed, wanting the missionaries' blessings to be
theirs alone, is not certain. Eventually, in early 1823, the Broadbents
and Hodgsons arrived at the home of the Barolong at Makwassi on
the Vaal River.

Just as these missionaries had found the tribe to whom they
wanted to minister, a tribe as yet unreached by others, and they
were about to settle down to work, other difficulties arose. The
marauding tribes which had been set in motion by Tshaka's wars in
Zululand set off other marauding tribes, one of which (the

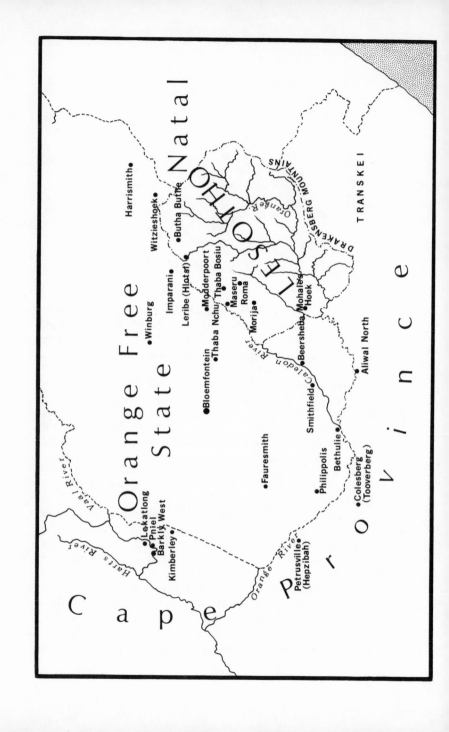

Bafokeng) was heading directly toward the Barolong on the Vaal River. Hodgson and his family had gone to Griqua Town to buy supplies, leaving Broadbent, who was still something of an invalid, and his wife and two small children, one only a few weeks old, at Maquassi. When the Barolong heard of the approach of the Batlokwa (thought to be the Mantatees) they took off to hide in the hills. Sifonelo, the chief, urged Broadbent and his family to flee with them, but since the missionary was very weak, and there were no oxen remaining, this was impossible. For several weeks Broadbent and his family lived alone (even the Griquas and Korannas who had been with them fled), with the possibility of attack imminent. But just in time, Hodgson returned and rescued the Broadbents. They returned to Griqua Town, and during their absence the mission station at Maquassi was destroyed by the Bataung people. When the missionaries discovered the destruction on their return, they helped the tribe settle at a new site on the Vaal River. But the area where the Barolong were living was congested as a result of the movements of tribes, and there were not enough grass and water. In 1833, after nearly a decade of mission work among the Barolong, the missionaries led the people to a new area about one hundred and fifty miles to the east. Here, at Thaba Nchu, the Methodists built a new community for the Barolong, on land which Moshesh, the Basotho chief, ceded to them. Later, some of the Barolong returned to the Vaal River area and to Mafeking; a Methodist missionarv accompanied them. Methodism has from this time been the church of the Barolong people.

From Thaba Nchu other Methodist mission stations spread out along the western side of the Caledon River valley. Some of these were branches of Thaba Nchu with Barolong people and others had Korannas and Griquas, but those to the northeast, nearer the mountains, were the first mission stations among the remnants of the Batlokwa people. Sikonyela, the chief of the Batlokwa, paid tribute to Dingane, the successor to Tshaka. The Rev. James Allison was founder of Imparani, the mission among the Batlokwa. He was present when Piet Retief and the other Boers went to Sikonyela to demand the cattle which Dingane claimed had been stolen from him. If it had not been for Allison, the Boers might have taken Sikonyela back to Dingane with them, as well as the cattle. Allison's fame in connection with this event spread far and some months later a delegation from a chief in Swaziland arrived at Imparani to beg

Allison to open a mission station in their territory. By the time the delegation arrived, a measles epidemic had taken a heavy toll among Sikonyela's people (as it did throughout Southern Africa in 1839 and 1840). One of the converts to Christianity was pointed out by the diviners as the source of the scourge, and he was put to death. Allison and the other converts evacuated Imparani, at first to Thaba Nchu, but later to Swaziland. Therefore the first mission to Swaziland grew out of this mission to the Batlokwa, and some of the Batlokwa converts took part in it.

Of all the mission stations in the Orange Free State, Thaba Nchu is the best known, because it was the place where the various groups of trekkers came together in 1837 and 1838. There they elected officials and drew up their first, rudimentary constitution for a republic. The Rev. James Archbell was helpful to many of the trekkers, and Moroka, the Barolong chief, rescued Potgieter's party after Mzilikazi had stolen their cattle. It was from Thabu Nchu that the trekkers split up, some going with Piet Retief and Gerrit Maritz to Natal, some going with Potgieter to the Transvaal, and others staying just north of Thaba Nchu at Winburg.

Probably it was because of these associations of Thaba Nchu with the Great Trek that the Barolong people retained the land during the next few decades when the Boers took more and more terrain, eventually taking all north and west of the Caledon River and even a portion south of the Caledon in the area near the confluence of the Caledon and Orange Rivers.

During the later 1840's there were wars between the Barolong (or some of them) and the Basotho, as well as between the Batlokwa and the Basotho. During one of these, a group of Barolong attacked the mission station at Umpukani, where there were Fingoes as well as Korannas, Griquas, and other Batswana. Those inhabitants who did not manage to get to the mission house were butchered in their homes, and even those in the mission house were shot at. The mission family (the Schreiners, the family of the novelist Olive Schreiner) had to walk twenty-four miles to the nearest mission station, and after they left everything was destroyed. Not only the station at Umpukani but other Methodist missions as well were closed during this period of fighting.

A quarter of a century later, of the original mission stations only Thaba Nchu remained on the list of churches in the Bechuana District, although work was being carried on in the towns which

were growing up — Bloemfontein, Smithfield, Fauresmith, and
Kimberley. In these places Methodist work included churches for
whites as well as for the non-whites, who had been the first object of
attention in the area. The Volksraad (legislature) of the Orange Free
State voted grants to the Methodist ministers in Bloemfontein,
Smithfield, and Fauresmith. The pattern of work that developed was
that of a white minister who lived in one of the towns and served
English-speaking whites while also supervising several African
catechists and evangelists. No African Methodist ministers were
ordained until the last quarter of the nineteenth century.

The trekkers who moved into the Free State area (also known as
Transorangia) were largely of Dutch background, but they did not
all agree on religious matters. In the northeastern Cape there had
been a significant number of farmers known as Doppers. Their
distinctive religious position involved singing only psalms in church,
simple forms of worship, and preference for outdated styles of
clothing. When the trekkers gathered at Thaba Nchu, religion was a
source of friction among them. None of the clergy of the Dutch
Reformed Church in the Cape was willing to go with the trekkers.
The trekkers, however, were eager to continue their religious
practices. Some wanted to ask Mr. Archbell of the Methodists to
become their pastor, but the majority wanted Mr. Erasmus Smit,
though he was not ordained. Mr. Smit had served as a London
missionary at one of the Bushman mission stations, and when it was
disbanded, had become a teacher in the Cape. Since there were no
clergy to ordain Smit, he read both the questions and the answers to
the service of ordination. After that, he administered the sacraments
and did all the usual work of a minister. Those who went to Natal
accepted Smit as their leader until, in 1840, they were able to get
the Reverend Daniel Lindley, an American missionary, to serve as
their pastor. Lindley moved to Pietermaritzburg, the capital of the
Boer Republic of Natal, and from there made lengthy journeys into
the Free State and Transvaal to administer the sacraments and do as
much pastoral work as was possible under the circumstances.
Lindley continued to serve the Boers as pastor until 1846, when the
British took over Natal; then went back to work with the Zulus.

In October 1847 the Dutch Reformed Synod in the Cape
appointed a commission to investigate conditions north of the
Orange River. They found no schools and only one consistory, at
Winburg. As a result of the work of this commission, consistories

were organized at Smithfield, Harrismith, and Bloemfontein, and in 1849 and 1850 pastors were sent to Bloemfontein and Winburg. The first to be sent to Bloemfontein was the Rev. Andrew Murray, Junior. His father had been one of several ministers of the Church of Scotland who had been sent to fill the needs of the Dutch Reformed churches at the Cape during the 1820's. The progeny of the Murray family were to fill many pulpits and provide many of the first missionaries of the Dutch Reformed Church.

The younger Andrew Murray, after serving for some years in Bloemfontein, and throughout the Orange Free State, moved to the Cape, where he led in the efforts to engage the Dutch Reformed Church in missionary activity among non-whites. He also founded a training school for missionaries at Wellington in the Cape. By 1878 there were eighteen Dutch Reformed congregations in the Free State. Many of these white congregations eventually developed "daughter churches" comprised of the non-white people of their communities. Impetus in this direction increased after the Anglo-Boer War of 1899-1902; among the Boer prisoners of war in Ceylon and St. Helena there occurred religious revivals which led many of the men to study the Bible seriously and to commit themselves to work for the conversion of non-whites after the war. Some of these prisoners became full-time missionaries, others worked in their own communities and supported the missionary effort.

At the request of the local chief, a mission of the Dutch Reformed Church was started at Witzie's Hoek, in the southeastern corner of the Free State, and eventually a theological school for Africans was built there. In the later part of the nineteenth century, the missionaries of the Paris Mission and those of the DRC agreed that the Paris Mission would not work in the Free State but would encourage those of its people who went to work and live there to join the DRC mission churches. For the Basotho Christians this was not always satisfactory, and eventually some of them organized themselves into churches which were accepted into membership in the Congregational Union.

Interspersed among the Methodist mission stations in the Caledon River valley were several stations of the Paris Mission. These stations were primarily for Basotho people, and when the Free State went to war against the Basotho, these stations were taken over. The land was divided up into farms for the Free Staters, and the people either moved into what is now Lesotho or became farm employees on the Free State farms. This expropriation of Paris Mission stations took place during the 1850's and 1860's.

On the western side of the Orange Free State, another group of missionaries, those of the Berlin Missionary Society, began work among some of the Koranna people. They had the usual difficulties in getting the people to settle down in one place rather than follow their usual nomadic habits. A portion of Jan Bloem's tribe of Koranna-Bastaards did, however, settle at Pniel, on the Vaal River near the site of the diamond diggings. What had been a quiet mission station came to be an urban slum, where the mixed-breed people of the earlier days mixed with the luckless whites cast off by the Kimberley diamond rush.

Though Archdeacon Merriman several times visited the Orange River Sovereignty (as it was known during the period of British rule from 1848 to 1854), walking from Grahamstown to Bloemfontein and back, and a deacon served the church at Bloemfontein for a few years during the 1850's, the Anglican Church was not really established in the Orange Free State until a bishop was consecrated and the area declared a diocese in 1863. A few years before, the consecration of a bishop for the territory bordering the Zambesi River had caused considerable debate about whether an Anglican bishop could be consecrated for a territory not included in the British Empire, but Bishop Mackenzie had been consecrated and went to martyrdom in what is now Malawi. Two years later, Bishop Twells was consecrated Bishop of Bloemfontein with the Orange Free State as his diocese. He took three priests with him. In addition to organizing congregations of whites in Bloemfontein and elsewhere, Bishop Twells entered into negotiations with Chief Moshoeshoe and Chief Moroka about missionary work among their people. This put him into conflict with the French missionaries and the Methodists, because the Methodists considered the Barolong their sphere of activity and the French missionaries considered the Basotho theirs. The Anglicans had the advantage of claiming to be the church of the powerful queen; Moshoeshoe was especially anxious to have an alliance with England and hoped that the Anglicans could help him achieve this. Moshoeshoe and Moroka both sent sons to Anglican schools, even to England, at the expense of the Anglican Church. But the diocese did not have the money to follow through very far in the Bishop's plans for mission work.

Bishop Twells, like most of the clergy in South Africa, was a high churchman and his plans for missionary development were based on the use of religious orders. An order for men, the Society of St. Augustine, was founded at Modderpoort; the priests of the Society worked among the Basotho in the Free State and in Lesotho, as well as providing services for the scattered white Anglicans in the southeastern part of the Free State. The Society of St. Augustine had difficulty in recruiting new men after the original impulse, and eventually the Modderpoort establishment was turned over to the Society of the Sacred Mission. A mission to the Barolong at Thaba Nchu was also started in the time of Bishop Twells. The bishop himself traveled widely and attempted to serve even the few scattered Anglicans in the Transvaal by itinerating among them. The equilibrium of the diocese was considerably shaken by charges of homosexuality made against the bishop, who fled the country. Bishop Webb, the next bishop, founded an order for women, who undertook educational and nursing work in the diocese of Bloemfontein. When Webb was translated to Grahamstown, he also started a religious order for women there.

In 1851 the first Roman Catholic priest went to work in the Orange Free State (or Orange River Sovereignty). He was Father Hoenderwangers, a Flemish priest and member of the Order of Premonstratensians, who had been recruited by Bishop Devereux of the Eastern Cape to work among Dutch-speaking South Africans. Father Hoenderwangers was an extremely energetic priest who ministered to Catholic soldiers among the British troops stationed at Bloemfontein when he first arrived and found parishioners among both the Dutch- and English-speaking people of the Free State, and even across the Vaal River in the Potchefstroom area. A year after he went to Bloemfontein, Father Hoenderwangers was transferred to the authority of Bishop Allard of Natal, though it was not until a number of years later that Bishop Allard got around to visiting the Free State.

On returning to Natal from that visit, Bishop Allard detoured into Lesotho and made the contacts which led to his most successful enterprise, the OMI (Oblates of Mary Immaculate) mission to the Basotho. Father Hoenderwangers continued to itinerate throughout the Free State until 1869, when an accident in which he broke both legs forced him to return to his monastery in Belgium. By 1870 practically all of the Catholics in the Free State had moved to

Kimberley because of the diamond rush. The two priests assigned to the Free State moved there, too. One was Father Hidien, who died of typhus in 1871 while running a tent hospital during a typhus epidemic. The other was Father LeBihan, who built many wood and iron churches and organized schools for white and non-white children. The Convent of the Holy Family opened a school in Bloemfontein in 1877 and in Kimberley the next year. The Orange Free State became a Vicariate in 1886, with Bishop Gaughren the first bishop; his headquarters were in Kimberley.

Father Hoenderwangers found that his parishioners shared the colour prejudices of their neighbors, and wrote to Bishop Allard about the problem. Allard's reply is still the position of the Catholic Church in South Africa, in spite of continuing prejudice on the part of some of its members: "As to colour the Catholic Church does not pay attention to it. Jesus Christ died for all without distinction."

# VIII

# LESOTHO

The work of the LMS among the Griquas and the Batswana north of the Orange River was the jumping-off place for mission work farther to the north and east. The Paris Evangelical Mission Society, whose first missionaries went out to South Africa at the invitation of Dr. Philip, visited Robert Moffat at Kuruman and from there went to Mosega to work among the Bahurutsi, a group of Batswana who were vassals of other Batswana tribes. But the depredations of Mzilikazi broke up the mission station at Mosega, the Bahurutsi were scattered, and the missionaries moved southwest, closer to Kuruman, where some of the remnants were collected at a new station called Motito. This work was continued by the Paris Mission for several decades, but eventually was taken over by the LMS. Just after the destruction of Mosega, three new missionaries arrived, Casalis, Arbousset, and Gosselin. Providentially, a new opportunity presented itself at that time: Moshoeshoe, the chief of the Basotho, who had gathered in the Maluti mountains to escape the marauding Zulus, asked one of the Griqua Christians of Philippolis that missionaries be sent to him. So the three new missionaries of the Paris Mission went to Moshoeshoe's village in Lesotho.

Moshoeshoe, whose people were a mixture of many tribes huddled together in the mountains for protection, had his headquarters on the mountain called Thaba Bosiu. This mountain was large enough and flat enough on top to allow many to stay there throughout sieges. The area afforded sufficient water, grass, and garden space, and the rocks on the precipices had in the past provided good ammunition to hurl down against enemies. This fortification saved the Basotho from the Zulus and later from the Boers. But it did not provide enough agricultural area for the kind of mission station that the missionaries envisaged. Therefore Moshoeshoe helped them find an area which would be suitable; the place chosen was Morija, about twenty-five miles southwest of Thaba Bosiu. Here the Paris missionaries struggled to build a house, plant gardens, and establish flocks. Their enemies were the Korannas, who still threatened the area with their horses and guns, and the wild animals which killed their flocks and invaded their gardens. Within a few years, however, stone houses, walled gardens with flourishing fruit trees, and school and church buildings clearly marked the spot as a mission station.

Moshoeshoe had promised that he would move near to Morija when the threats of war had disappeared. He did send his son and a large group of people to live there, but he himself continued to feel that the protection of the nation demanded his presence on Thaba Bosiu. Casalis then established a second mission station in the valley below Thaba Bosiu. Moshoeshoe attended church there each Sunday and entered into long and knowledgeable discussions of theology, but he did not become a member of the church until many years later, on his deathbed.

The Basotho were very interested in the teaching of the missionaries, but by no means always agreed with it, particularly not when the missionaries criticized the customs of the people. By the late 1830's there were already chiefs and people known for their opposition to Christianity. Moshoeshoe, it would appear, was greatly attracted to it, and certainly attracted to his missionary, Casalis, but was afraid the tribe would be seriously disrupted if he were to publicly accept the Christian faith. There were difficulties over the burials of the first Christians, because many feared that if the proper rituals were not followed the whole tribe would suffer. They feared the wrath of the ancestors.

By the late 1830's a new threat had arisen in Lesotho. The Boers had left the Cape, had crossed the Orange River, and were beginning to stake out farms in what is now the Orange Free State. The southern and western parts of the Orange Free State are dry and suitable only for pastoral farming. But the eastern parts have more rainfall and are suitable for wheat and corn, as well as for cattle and sheep. Naturally, the white farmers were attracted to the better watered parts. In the Caledon River valley they came into contact with the Basotho and Batswana refugees who had settled there with the Methodist and Paris missionaries. When there had been war the Basotho had retreated back into the mountains south of the Caledon River, but whenever there was security they moved down into the valley, where they grew their crops. A conflict over this desirable farm land was inevitable. And from the 1840's until 1868 there was war, on and off, between the Boers and the Basotho. If the British had not declared Lesotho a protectorate in 1868, the Boers would probably have eventually taken over all of Lesotho. As it was, more than half of the agricultural land was lost to the Free State farmers, and the country was disrupted by war for many years.

The hopeful prospects the missionaries had in the 1830's waned with long years of fighting, then poverty and malnutrition. Even after the protectorate was declared, it was uncertain whether the Colonial Office in Britain or the government of the Cape Colony would administer Lesotho. Ever mindful of opportunities to save money, the Colonial Office passed the responsibility over to the Cape government.

Fearing war from all sides, the Cape government passed a law saying that no Africans could own guns. Yet within the ten years previous to this, the promise of guns had been held out to them to encourage them to work on the diamond mines in Kimberley. The guns which had been sold to them in Kimberley were obsolete, but they had been sold at high prices. Now, in 1880, they were told they must turn in their guns and be compensated less than half what they had paid because the guns were obsolete. The result of this was the Gun War in 1880 and 1881.

The French missionaries commiserated with the Basotho and protested to the Cape government and Colonial Office (one of the main complaints was that the Basotho had never been consulted about their administration's having been transferred to the Cape); their counsel to the Basotho, however, was not to go to war about it. When some of the Basotho did go to war, the French missionaries were accused of having incited the war. Their mission stations were occupied by Cape troops and their activities made impossible.

The biggest problem, besides the destruction and death resulting from the war, was the split which it caused among the Basotho people. The most adamant Basotho blamed the missionaries for having gotten them into trouble because the missionaries had advised Moshoeshoe to beg for a protectorate. Church members themselves were divided between fighting and not fighting. By this time there were Roman Catholic and Anglican missions in Lesotho as well. John Widdicombe, the Anglican missionary in the north, became chaplain to the Cape troops and clearly identified with that side in the war. The Roman Catholics managed to stay neutral throughout. But the Paris missionaries became the enemies of the Cape even though they attempted to counsel peace to their people. Those Christians who went to war were not excommunicated, as had happened during earlier fighting. But there were deep scars in the church as well in Basotho society because of the divisions caused by the war and the circumstances surrounding it. The hope of the earlier Paris missionaries that there might be a national church of the Basotho faded because of the war, as well as because of the presence of missionaries of other denominations.

Such tribal customs as ritual murder, which had receded into the mountain fastnesses, if they had not disappeared completely, came into prominence again during the war and the period of dislocation following it. The liquor traffic, which had been declared illegal by Moshoeshoe, grew from smuggling occasional bottles of brandy to openly importing barrels. Moshoeshoe's own son drank openly. This was a cause of great despair to the missionaries.

Nevertheless, the church grew in the period following the war. The complete Bible in Sesotho had been printed, theological training had been developed, the number and extent of schools grew rapidly, including the teacher-training program at Morija, and the organization of parishes and the synod began. Perhaps because the hope of the first-generation missionaries for a national church had failed, or perhaps in reaction to the methods of the Roman Catholics, who were beginning to send large numbers of missionaries to Lesotho, the Paris missionaries in the last two decades of the nineteenth century emphasized the necessity of a long trial before membership and the necessity of purity on the part of members. The Church of the Paris Mission became an elite of morality and of education.

During the early 1860's, Bishop Allard, the Roman Catholic bishop of Natal and other interior places, toured the Orange Free State. He visited Molapo, a son of Moshoeshoe who lived in the north of Lesotho, and received from him a cordial welcome, which led the bishop to hope that he might be received by Moshoeshoe as well. Bishop Allard and priests of the Oblates of Mary Immaculate had been sent out from France as a missionary order, but their only success to this point had been among whites in Natal. Their efforts among the Zulus had been a failure. Therefore, they were eager to find a field where their missionary work might take root. Lesotho offered opportunities for combating both heathenism and Protestantism.

In his interview with Moshoeshoe in 1862, Bishop Allard emphasized the biblical basis of Catholic doctrine, a criterion with which the Basotho were familiar. He promised that if the Catholics were permitted to open a mission station, they would teach reading and writing, weaving and sewing. On this basis, the site which is now Roma, about twenty miles south of Thaba Bosiu, was granted to the Catholics. Father Gerard, who had accompanied Bishop Allard, was the pioneer missionary.

Bishop Allard and Father Gerard treated Moshoeshoe as they would have treated the King of France and always emphasized the authority of the chief. During the war with the Orange Free State in the 1860's, Father Gerard helped starving Basotho, even helping Moshoeshoe with badly needed provisions. In 1865 the Sisters of the Holy Family arrived, to make good Bishop Allard's promise to teach the Basotho how to weave and sew. Their first work, however, was to nurse the wounded and starving during the war. Organizing an orphanage was also one of their first concerns. At first, the Basotho were not eager to send their daughters to school, because the Catholic missionaries were opposed to polygamy. But eventually this distrust was overcome, though girls from heathen families seldom were sent to school.

Father Gerard made it easy for the Basotho who became interested in Catholicism to exhibit that allegiance even though the degree of their involvement was slight. He invented greetings which Catholic adherents used with one another wherever they went, and distributed crucifixes widely, so that many who wore almost no clothes still wore a crucifix. Though the number of baptized converts was small until the twentieth century, the number of adherents who felt themselves to have a relationship to the Catholic Church grew rapidly. But these people were only gradually weaned away from the tribal customs of their ancestors. And for baptized Catholics, penance rather than excommunication was the usual result of failure to live up to the Christian standards taught by the missionaries. Public penance was established by Father Gerard, and even he underwent it on occasion.

Why did Moshoeshoe permit the Roman Catholic missionaries to enter Lesotho? Presumably the Protestant missionaries objected, but the force of their objections may not have been too strong. Moshoeshoe's near neighbor, Eugene Casalis, had just before (1860) been named head of the missionary training center in Paris. Furthermore, throughout the late 1850's and 1860's, the Paris missionaries were worried mainly about the Boers of the Orange Free State; it looked highly probable that they would defeat the Basotho and that the Paris missionaries would be forced out, as they had been from stations in the Free State. Father W. E. Brown, a Catholic historian, suggests that the involvements of the Paris missionaries with the politics of some of the local chiefs was a factor, perhaps also Moshoeshoe's distaste for the domineering kind of wife who seemed to accompany the Paris missionaries. It is even more likely to suppose that Moshoeshoe felt that his power would be safer with more than one mission group in his country — their vying with each other would enhance his own position. This explanation best reveals, too, why Moshoeshoe delayed until his deathbed his own baptism, though he was obviously converted to Christianity much earlier.

The first visit of an Anglican was even earlier than that of Bishop Allard, but Bishop Gray's visit to Moshoeshoe in 1850 was not followed up effectively until the 1870's. In 1875 Father Stenson went to Mohale's Hoek in the south and Canon Widdicombe went to Leribe (Hlotse) in the north. A few years before this, an Anglican community, the Society of the Sacred Mission, had established a mission at Modderpoort in the Free State, just across the Caledon River from Lesotho. At Modderpoort the Anglicans began to develop liturgical services and other patterns which were also followed in Lesotho. When Widdicombe arrived at Leribe, he was greeted by Chief Molapo, a son of Moshoeshoe:

> A chief liked to have many cows: the more he had the more milk he got, and the better he was able to feed his children. Now he should have three cows, all of them of excellent breed in their way, and yielding an abundance of milk. At first he had only one cow, the French Protestant Mission. Quite lately, only a month ago, he had acquired another cow, the Roman

Catholic Mission; for he had just given permission to M. Gerard to commence a mission at the Komokoana; and now today he was to have a third, and perhaps the best cow of all; for was not this new cow a present from the Queen of England herself? Now he was happy. He not only had a black cow, and a dun one, but today a red one also was to enter his kraal.[1]

Within a few years another station was started in the north at Butha Buthe. At Easter 1877 the first converts, three Basotho and one Zulu, were baptized. There were so many enquirers that the church had to be expanded. The Anglican missionaries served the traders and government servants who came to Lesotho, as well as the Basotho. Their emphasis was on worship. The first service, held at Leribe in 1876, began with an invocation to the Trinity and continued with an acknowledgement of sin, a hymn, a chapter from one of the Gospels and a discourse upon it, the Agnus Dei, the Good Friday collect for the conversion of the heathen, the prayer of S. Chrysostom, and the Grace. How the Basotho reacted to this is not recorded. The center of attraction in the church was a painting of the crucifixion at Calvary; crowds came to see and comment on this. The Gun War broke out just a few years after the beginning of the Anglican missions. Canon Widdicombe told his people to turn in their guns to the government. As a result, the mission station was destroyed, after being used as a fort by the colonial soldiers, and the Anglican converts were considered traitors by other Basotho.

In the 1880's the missionaries began to notice that people were living permanently in the mountainous areas where previously they had only grazed their animals at certain times of the year. Overpopulation was beginning. And the soil erosion which appears everywhere in Lesotho now began to be apparent in the fertile alluvial plains. As the soil was washed down the rivers, the land was left deeply scarred. Too many people and too little level ground for planting — greatly intensified by the acquisitions of the Boer farmers — meant that what land was left had to be overworked. Malnutrition became a perpetual problem, where earlier it had been a problem only in time of war. Kimberley and Johannesburg offered possibilities for employment, and imported food became an expensive stop-gap for the loss of fertile lands.

Since its inception, the Church of the Paris Mission had been pushing farther into the mountain areas of Lesotho. But in the 1870's an opportunity to send Basotho missionaries much farther afield appeared. The Swiss Reformed churches had been contributing to the Paris Society, but wished to organize a mission of their own. Some Basotho evangelists accompanied the Swiss missionaries across the Transvaal territory and into what in now Rhodesia. The Swiss Mission decided to open a mission in the northern Transvaal, but the Basotho hoped to have their own mission effort to the Banyai. The Banyai were subject to Lobengula, the Ndebele chief, and he refused permission for missionaries to the Banyai; even before this difficulty there had been vicissitudes in the Transvaal, because the Boers considered the Basotho evangelists as troublemakers and put them in jail. Later a new party, with the missionary Coillard, went north through Botswana and found Sesotho-speaking people in the swamps of the Zambesi River. Here, among the Barotse and the Makalolo (descendants of the Bafokeng marauders), the Paris Society and the Basotho Church established a new mission.

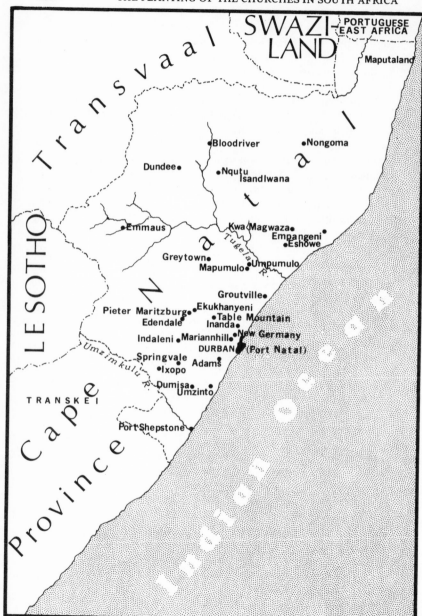

**SWAZI-LAND**

**PORTUGUESE EAST AFRICA**

Transvaal

LESOTHO

Maputaland

Bloodriver• •Nongoma

Dundee•

•Nqutu
Isandlwana

Kwa •Magwaza•

•Emmaus

Empangeni•
•Eshowe

Greytown•

Umpumulo•

Mapumulo•

Natal

Groutville•

Pieter Maritzburg• •Ekukhanyeni

Edendale• •Table Mountain

Indaleni• Inanda•

•Mariannhill •New Germany

DURBAN (Port Natal)

Springvale•

Adams•

•Ixopo

•Dumisa•

Umzinto•

TRANSKEI

Cape

Port Shepstone•

Province

Tugela R.

Umzimkulu R.

Indian Ocean

# IX

# NATAL

In 1824 a group of traders from the Grahamstown area opened up business at Port Natal (Durban). Ivory was what they wanted most, and in order to get it they had to sell guns and ammunition to the Zulus, though they also had a good trade in blankets, beads, and cooking pots, plus exotic military-type uniforms and such for important chiefs like Tshaka and Dingane. Tshaka himself granted these traders land rights at Port Natal, and under Dingane they got grants of land extending along the coast north and south of the port. Some of the traders set themselves up as chiefs with Zulus who had run away from Zululand as their supporters. Some had many African wives and created whole new tribes of mixed-breed people. The land and authority which the traders were able to acquire were secured not only because of their technological superiority, but also because of the anarchy which followed in the wake of the tyrant Tshaka. The population of large tracts of Natal had been decimated by Tshaka, and the few survivors were living in inaccessible valleys. Into this vacuum first the traders, then the Boer trekkers, came (1838).

One of the traders had as interpreter a Xhosa who had spent some time in jail in Grahamstown. This man told the Zulu chief that the experience of the Xhosas had been that the first white man who came talked about a book and about God, but that other men, who inevitably followed after, were soldiers who took away the land. The first missionary to talk about the Book at the Zulu royal kraal was Captain Allan Gardiner, a retired British naval officer who became a missionary after his wife's death. Captain Gardiner arrived in Natal in 1835. After a number of visits to Zululand he concluded that permanent success in mission work could not be accomplished until some kind of law and order was imposed on the white traders at Port Natal. With the support of a few of these traders, but certainly not of all, Gardiner returned to England to try to persuade the British government to make Natal a British colony (or extend the Cape Colony to include Natal) and also to seek support from the Church Missionary Society for his enterprise.

In the latter objective, he succeeded in bringing back with him in 1837 the Rev. Francis Owen and his family; and another mission worker arrived the next year. With regard to the former objective, Gardiner was appointed magistrate by the British government, but the area was not proclaimed British and Gardiner was given no funds and no police or militia to back up his authority. By the force of moral persuasion he was supposed to keep a group of elephant hunters and gun runners in line. This, as Gardiner found out, was impossible. The whole situation broke down completely when the Boer trekkers, led by Piet Retief, arrived in Natal to take over what they considered their promised land.

When Retief and a party of about sixty men, mostly Boers but accompanied by a few English-speaking Port Natal traders, visited Dingane a second time to consummate the treaty which he had promised on the first visit, a treaty which granted the Boers all the land south of the Tugela River, Dingane ordered all the whites massacred. Following this, the trekker parties which had camped at the foot of the Drakensberg mountains were attacked and many killed. During the year 1838 a number of battles were fought between the Zulus and the trekkers, the Zulus keeping the upper hand until the Battle of Blood River in December 1838, when Dingane was decisively beaten. During 1839 the Boers took over the whole of Natal, leaving the territory north of the Tugela to Mpande, Dingane's brother, who had become a stooge of the Boers as well as Dingane's successor to the Zulu throne.

Captain Gardiner was not the only one who had seen that the Zulus needed missionaries. During the early 1830's Dr. John Philip had been corresponding with the American Board of Commissioners for Foreign Missions about sending missionaries to the two branches of the Zulu people — Dingane's people in Zululand and Mzilikazi's people in the Transvaal. The American Board was

an interdenominational society supported by American Congregationalists and Presbyterians, as well as by a few smaller church
bodies (after 1870 it became a solely Congregational body). As a
result of Philip's invitation, the American Board recruited a
group of six couples, three to go to Mzilikazi's people (Rev. and Mrs.
Daniel Lindley, Rev. and Mrs. Henry Venable, and Dr. and Mrs.
Alexander Wilson) and three to go to Zululand (Rev. and Mrs. Aldin
Grout, Rev. and Mrs. George Champion, and Dr. and Mrs. Newton
Adams). They left Boston in December 1834 and the Zululand
group arrived at Port Natal a year later, after spending time for
orientation in Cape Town with Dr. Philip and at Bethelsdorp, held
up by the war between the British and the Xhosas (the War of
1835).

The year 1836 was spent in exploration, visits to Dingane,
returning to Port Elizabeth and Bethelsdorp for their wives (Mrs.
Grout died at Bethelsdorp in February 1836), obtaining supplies,
and other preparations for work. By the end of 1837, Lindley,
Venable, and Wilson had joined the three in Natal, because the
Boers' defeat of Mzilikazi had made their mission impossible. With
six men and four women (Mrs. Wilson had died in the Transvaal),
and four mission sites (two in Zululand and two in Natal) the
prospects for mission work looked good. A printing press had been
imported, and serious work was being done to reduce Zulu to
writing and to produce school materials, as well as portions of the
Bible and hymns. Great crowds gathered for preaching, especially in
Natal where people sometimes walked for long distances to hear the
new teaching. Schools were also started. In Zululand it was more
difficult. Dingane often made it difficult for people to talk to the
missionaries, and his support for the missionaries was sporadic at
best. In general, however, the outlook was good.

The massacre of Retief's party and the wars which followed threw
everything into confusion. The missionaries in Zululand considered
their position impossible and so returned to Port Natal. Mr. Owen
had observed the massacre and Venable came upon the scene soon
after. When the Zulus invaded Natal, all the missionaries except
Lindley and Owen went by sea to Port Elizabeth, and somewhat
later Lindley and Owen also left. When the American Board heard
about the events in Zululand, they ordered the mission closed, but it
took so long to communicate back and forth that by the time the
order was received, matters looked more hopeful and Lindley and

Adams refused to return to America. The Venables and Champions did return to America, where both Champions died within a few years. Dr. Wilson remarried in America and then became a pioneer in the mission at Cape Palmas in West Africa. Aldin Grout also remarried in America, but returned to South Africa where he spent most of the remainder of his life. Dr. Newton Adams went back to Port Natal and lived on his income as a medical practitioner until the American Board agreed to reopen the mission. Lindley preached in Port Elizabeth and organized the first Temperance Society there, but in 1839 he, too, returned to Port Natal, where he started a school for Boer children. The next year he accepted the call of the trekkers to be their pastor in Pietermaritzburg and inland.

In 1840, too, Aldin Grout returned. From May 1841 to July 1842 the Grouts worked at a place where Empangeni in Zululand now is. At first it seemed that he had Mpande's support, but he soon discovered that it was only because Mpande feared the whites that he had permitted the Grouts to live there. As people began to show an interest in Grout's teaching, Mpande's feelings turned to distinct opposition. And when Mpande confiscated the property of the converts and threatened their lives, the Grouts, along with their converts, left Zululand and built south of the Tugela River, on the banks of the Umvoti River (the mission station known as Groutville). In 1843 the British government annexed Natal. It took a long time before the annexation was effective, but by 1845 most of the Boers had withdrawn to the highveld and British administration began to operate. In the late 1840's Adams established what is now known as Adams' Mission on the Amamzimtoti River, Lindley started work among the Amaqadi people at Umzinyati (later he moved to a more healthful site at Inanda), and Grout continued his work on the Umvoti. The first baptism took place at Amamzimtoti, when Mbulasi, a woman who had fled from Zululand when her husband, a chief, was killed by Tshaka, and had lived with the Adams family for some years, confessed her faith. By 1850 there were thirty-two church members at Amamzimtoti, where Mbulasi assisted Dr. Adams in visiting homes and leading prayer meetings and generally helped to bring the people of the Makhanya tribe to know Christ.

The peace and order which came with the British administration also brought new immigrants from Britain. Throughout the 1850's the matter most on the minds of the missionaries — Adams (who died in 1851), Grout, and Lindley, plus fifteen new couples who were sent out from America from 1846 to 1860 — was securing land for the Africans. The new immigrants, and the few Boer families who remained in Natal, claimed that all the land should be available to them. Fortunately, Adams and Lindley were appointed to the Land Commission, along with Theophilus Shepstone, Secretary for Native Affairs, and Lieutenant Gibbs of the Royal Engineers. By the time the Land Commission had done its work, most of the best land for agriculture had already been taken by the white farmers, but six tribal locations were set apart in Natal by 1855. In 1856 Sir George Grey, governor of the Cape, granted glebes to the mission societies that were then at work in Natal and mission reserves around the glebes, to provide secure tenure to the Africans who wanted to live near the missionaries. Twelve of these glebes and mission reserves were allotted to the American Board, while one or two each were given to the Anglicans, Lutherans, Methodists, and Catholics. Some of these were not retained; while at one point twenty-one were proposed, in 1903 there were only seventeen.

Whether one gives primacy to the Anglicans or to the American Board, the third group was definitely the Norwegian Lutherans and the fourth the Methodists. The first Lutheran missionary was Hans P. S. Schreuder, a Norwegian, who arrived in 1844 to open a mission station near Mpande's village. He could not obtain permission for this, however, and he left South Africa for a time, going to the Far East, where China appealed to him as a mission field. His red hair, however, made him an unsuitable missionary to the Chinese. In 1848 he returned to South Africa, where other Norwegians joined him. In 1850 they started mission work at Umpumulo, with the hope that Mpande's country, north of the Tugela, might open to them soon. This did happen within a few years, when Schreuder was called upon to treat Mpande during an illness. During the 1860's several Norwegian mission stations were opened in Zululand. But no converts were made until the 1880's; Zulus who became interested in the gospel either had to flee to Natal or face death from one of Mpande's men. This was also true under Cetshwayo, Mpande's successor. The Lutheran, and later Anglican, mission stations continued in this very difficult position in spite of the obstacles because they did have some opportunities to teach children and because occasionally women were able to stay on the mission stations. This problematic situation continued until after the defeat of the Zulus in the Zulu war of 1879. Real progress in Zululand did not come until Zululand was incorporated in the British Empire. It is perhaps understandable that the missionaries, the Anglicans in particular, created some of the public feeling toward Cetshwayo which urged the British officials on toward war in 1879 – a war they were not really prepared for, as is evident from the disaster of Isandlwana.

The Berlin Mission, which had already begun work among the Korannas on the Vaal River and in the Cape, sent the Rev. W. Posselt, who worked among the Zulus and German immigrants at New Germany, a few miles inland from Durban. Another Berlin Mission station was started at Emmaus in the foothills of the Drakensberg mountains near Bergville by a layman, Güldenpfennig, in 1846. The Rev. J. L. Döhne, who had served in the Eastern Cape, also went to Natal in 1846, but he soon accepted the pastorate of the Church of the Vow, the Dutch Reformed Church in Pietermaritzburg, when Lindley went back to work for the American Board. A few years later Döhne joined the American Board and worked at Table Mountain, near Pietermaritzburg, where he devoted much time preparing a Zulu dictionary.

A rather different type of Lutheran mission was that of the Hermannsburg Mission in the Natal midlands (near Greytown). In 1853 a group of artisans and clergy sponsored by the Hermannsburg Mission Society in Hanover, Germany, left Germany to go to Ethiopia, where they hoped to set up a Christian colony which would evangelize the Galla people, about whom Ludwig Krapf had written from his explorations in East Africa. They did not succeed in reaching the Gallas, however, so instead of returning to Germany, they landed in Natal and bought land on which to establish their Christian colony. The rule of the group was that all property should be owned in common, and the work of the farmers and artisans was to support those who could give full time to evangelizing the heathen. The colony prospered and a number of farms were purchased. The rule was found to be unworkable, however, and most of the farmers and artisans became independent colonists who continued to speak German and support the Hermannsburg church and its mission work.

During the last half of the nineteenth century, the Church of Sweden also undertook mission work in Natal and Zululand. Schreuder broke with the Norwegian Missionary Society and founded a group of mission stations on his own. These were later taken over by the American Lutherans. Another group was the Hanoverian Free Church Mission, the result of a split in the Hermannsburg Mission; later this too was largely taken over by American Lutherans (Buffalo Synod). Most of these Lutheran bodies sent representatives to a series of Lutheran conferences, starting in 1889; and this cooperation led to a joint hymnbook and a joint magazine in Zulu. Later this led further to the organization called the Cooperating Lutheran Missions in Natal and, eventually, to the Evangelical Lutheran Church.

It has often been the custom of Methodists to move their ministers frequently. The first Methodist minister appointed to Natal, James Archbell, had begun his ministry among the Namaquas. It is said he lost his usefulness by upbraiding the cowdung-smeared Namaquas for embracing his wife upon his arrival in the country. From Namaqualand he was sent to work among the Barolong, and from there to the Eastern Cape, where he served both English and Xhosas. In 1846 Archbell was appointed to Pietermaritzburg, Natal. In 1847 another Methodist also came to Pietermaritzburg. This was the Rev. Allison, with a following of Batlokwa and Swazi converts, after their flight from Swaziland. Allison pioneered two mission stations, first one at Indaleni and then one at Edendale (the latter he founded in his private capacity after he had severed his connection with the Methodists, though he encouraged his converts to stay within the Methodist Church). The men whom Allison brought with him, he trained as evangelists and teachers, and they were very effective in building up Methodist work throughout Natal.

At one time the Methodists and the American Board discussed comity arrangements, the American Board working in the coastal areas and the Methodists working in the interior, but the enthusiasm of the African Methodists made this impossible. Africans who went to the towns to work became involved in the closely organized class system of the Methodists; when they went home to the farms and locations they became organizers themselves. This type of organization suited the conditions so well that the church of the American Board, though Congregational in name, is organized on the same pattern, with every member being the responsibility of a class leader. The division of the members into classes and the choice of class leaders owes something to the traditional Zulu ideas of age-grade groupings, an unconscious form of indigenization.

When the Rev. Francis Owen, his sister, and Mr. Hewitson, who had arrived at Port Natal only in time to leave with the Owens, fled from Natal, Anglican activity stopped for about a decade. When Bishop Gray came to South Africa he sent James Green, later Dean of Pietermaritzburg, to Natal; there was also a colonial chaplain in Durban. Bishop Gray himself visited Natal, along with the rest of South Africa, and discussed with Green the possibilities for developing mission work. Their idea was that each of the African locations which were then being proposed should have a kind of community center in which a minister, school teacher, mechanic, farmer, and doctor would work. Bishop Colenso, who arrived in Natal in 1854, and Theophilus Shepstone, the Secretary for Native Affairs for Natal, agreed that this was a good plan. Sir George Grey, the Governor of the Cape, had similar ideas as a way to avoid future conflicts, such as had happened in the Eastern Cape. Sir George did make grants to a number of mission groups to enable them to operate industrial schools. But the British government was expected to foot the bill for these projects. Sir George tried to persuade the powers in London that this would be cheaper than wars, but the Little Englanders, who wanted to reduce overseas commitments as much as possible, were in the saddle in Parliament. Bishop Colenso himself, at Ekukanyeni, just outside Pietermaritzburg, undertook some of these projects. At Springvale in the Umkomaas River valley, Dr. Henry Callaway (who later became the first bishop of the Diocese of St. John's in the Transkei) attempted to build such a comprehensive mission station; Callaway was a medical practitioner as well as a priest, so he was particularly well fitted for such work. He also, like Colenso, was deeply engaged in linguistic and anthropological studies of Zulu culture. But by and large the scheme floundered for lack of capital, and the rural locations stagnated as the most able-bodied Africans were drawn off for labor, a practice necessitated by the tax policies of the colony of Natal. Under the guise of teaching Africans the dignity of labor, Natal managed to collect more taxes from native poll and hut taxes than from any other source.

For the first few years of Colenso's episcopacy, things augured well for the Anglicans in Natal. By 1858, however, a series of controversies began to emanate from the bishop's activities and his publications. While Bishop Gray and Dean Green, both of whom held Tractarian sentiments, concerned themselves with the Real

Presence in the Eucharist and attempted to build up a strong, well-organized Anglican church in South Africa, Bishop Colenso, a Broad Churchman who attempted to follow some of F. D. Maurice's insights and was intrigued by the critical biblical studies of the German theologians, was faced with problems of apologetics in presenting the gospel to Zulus. The first battle was between Green and Colenso over eucharistic theology; Gray upheld Colenso by acknowledging that his views were within the acceptable limits (though he really agreed with Green). After this, there was an argument over the constitution for a Diocesan Synod; many clergy were alienated by the bishop's suggestion that clergy and laity should sit together. Colenso's *Commentary on the Epistle to the Romans* (1861) brought serious conflict with Bishop Gray and most orthodox Christians. Another book soon afterwards presented Colenso's views on the authorship of the Pentateuch; it is hardly startling to modern readers, but was quite shocking to Victorian churchmen who had never doubted the total inerrancy of the Scriptures. Hearings were held in England and a heresy trial took place in Cape Town. Colenso was deposed as bishop. But an appeal to the Privy Council gave him the right to retain his see and all its property. Unfortunately, however, he had already lost practically all of his clergy and his laity. Spectacular episodes of partisans and principals locking each other out of churches, and so forth, took place. Colenso stuck it out until his death — continuing such scandalous activities as baptizing polygamists and defending chiefs who got in trouble with the colonial administration. An orthodox bishop was appointed (since Colenso was still legally Bishop of Natal, Macrorie was consecrated as Bishop of Maritzburg, which was considered to be a legal see since Maritzburg was not the legal name of the place). At great expense, the orthodox Anglicans bought property and built new church buildings, since Colenso still had control of the original properties. Some years after Colenso's death the largest part of the schism was healed, but a small group called the Church of England in South Africa still continues to have its own bishop and a few congregations; ironically it tends to be fundamentalist.

Like the Lutherans, the Anglicans had a grim time in Zululand until after the British take-over there. Then they grew rapidly. At Kwa Magwaza and at Nqutu large mission stations were developed. Schools and hospitals were established in both Natal and Zululand.

Zululand became a diocese in the late 1860's, endowed as a memorial to Bishop Mackenzie, the pioneer and martyr of the Universities' Mission to Central Africa. There had been constitutional difficulties in getting him consecrated, but once done, the constitutional problems worked themselves out, as the Province of South Africa began to work more or less smoothly under the Archbishop of Cape Town. Though congregations are usually divided by language, the Anglicans have always been organized on a multi-racial basis.

The Roman Catholics also began work in Natal in the 1850's. The first bishop, Bishop Allard, was a member of the Oblates of Mary Immaculate, originally a French order but in more recent years drawing many of its priests from Canada. Though Bishop Allard's primary responsibility was to convert the heathen, he found that realities made it necessary for him to give priority to supplying priests and buildings to the Roman Catholics in Durban and Pietermaritzburg. These early priests had language problems. They knew only French, while their parishioners were almost all English speaking. Furthermore, in order to carry out the mandate to do mission work they had to learn Zulu, but all the written materials to help them learn Zulu (such as Colenso's and Döhne's dictionaries and, later, Lewis Grout's grammar) were written in English. Bishop Allard had arrived in Natal in 1852, but he was short of clergy, so that it was not until 1855 that two priests were set aside to learn Zulu and open a mission station at Dumisa's (between Umzinto and Ixopo, in present-day terms). After four years, however, Bishop Allard closed this mission, concluding that the Zulus were too hardhearted. Soon afterward he turned his attentions to the Basotho.

In 1882, when the Trappists gave up their efforts in the Eastern Cape and moved to Natal, Roman Catholic missions to the Zulus really began in earnest. Father Pfanner, the Abbot of Mariannhill, collected 130 priests and brothers in four years. He raised money to build monasteries, farms, schools, and industrial projects; approaching a mission station of the Mariannhill Fathers, one feels that he is coming to a medieval European village. This was the model that was followed. Father Pfanner's idea of mission work was to build a Christian community first, then through participation in aspects of that community it was expected that the heathen would come to know and love Christ. The first monastery was built at Mariannhill, near Durban. But almost before this was finished, Pfanner was building others, some as far as two hundred miles away. Within a few years, it was quite clear that the Trappist rule was not suitable to this kind of mission work. Most members of the community were having to be excused from one or another part of the rule most of the time. The leaders of the Trappists in Europe were concerned about this state of affairs. At one time Abbot Pfanner was relieved of his office and disciplined. In the end, the only way around the problem was to create a new order with a new rule which would meet the needs of the missionary fathers. So the Religious Missionaries of Mariannhill became a separate order in 1909.

Farming was an important part of the Mariannhill mission work. As the order bought property for its stations, it became landlord to many Zulus, requiring of its tenants certain standards of agriculture and housing. The injunction to work was stressed to the extent that one of the abbots made a rule that baptismal candidates had to promise to do manual work. Tenants were required to build houses with upright walls (the traditional Zulu hut was of the beehive, upside-down basket, type), a door, and a window.

The emphasis on work went through the educational establishments as well. Religious, agricultural, and industrial training were the mainstays of the curriculum. Later, came teacher training and high school programs. An order of nuns, the Congregation of the Precious Blood, was established to give training to the girls. Later, a hospital was added to the Mariannhill complex. In the twentieth century one of the best known of the Mariannhill Fathers was Father Bernard Huss, who was famous for organizing cooperatives among Africans.

The southern part of Natal and much of the Transkei are included in the area served by the Mariannhill Fathers. In other parts of Natal, the Oblates of Mary Immaculate serve the African population as well as the whites. Father Mathieu was the pioneer of mission work along the north coast. With the help of the Dominican Sisters at Oakford, churches were established in many places, the spadework often done by African women who gathered the children of an area, taught them, and called Father Mathieu to come and examine them. The Oblates also served the Catholic Indians who came among the indentured sugar cane workers who started arriving in 1860. Later, Anglicans, Methodists, Lutherans, and the South Africa General Mission also turned their attention to the Indian population of Natal (nearly half of all the people in Durban are Indians). Pastor Rowland, who organized Bethesda Temple in Durban, and a number of branches, founded the largest Indian Christian group in Natal; his mission is an independent faith mission. In Zululand the Benedictines are responsible for the inland area, where they have a hospital at Nongoma and a school, Inkamana, at Vryheid. In the northeast of Zululand, where the people are not Zulus but Tongas, the American Servites have recently developed a number of missions.

By 1860 there were at work in Natal Anglicans, Congregationalists (American Board), Methodists, Lutherans, and Catholics. The Presbyterians, as the Free Church of Scotland Mission, also established themselves; the Rev. James Allison, who had broken with the Methodists, became one of their first missionaries. The Scandinavian Lutherans may have had something to do with the other Scandinavians who arrived later in the country: the Swedish Holiness Union Mission, the Scandinavian Alliance Mission, the Norwegian Free Mission, and the Scandinavian Baptist Union. The Salvation Army, the Free Methodists, the South African General Mission, and the Dutch Reformed Church all have mission work in Natal and Zululand also. The main station of the Dutch Reformed Church was built at Blood River in northern Zululand, the place where the Boers finally defeated the Zulus in December 1838. Natal is a small province and this multiplicity of mission societies makes it one of the most over-occupied mission fields in the world.

# X

# THE TRANSVAAL

In the early years of white contact with the territory north of the Vaal River, Mzilikazi, the Zulu leader who had fled from Tshaka and created his own Tshaka-like realm on the highveld, was the important figure. The tribes which had lived there previously — various Basotho and Batswana groups, primarily — had been pushed back into the mountains and deserts. Their villages in the good agricultural areas had been obliterated by Mzilikazi's group and the other marauding groups which had been sparked off by his invasions. Moffat, whose station at Kuruman was the missionary beachhead in the interior, met Mzilikazi and became his friend (the story of this friendship is one of the most interesting in South African mission history). Through this friendship, possibilities for establishing a mission at Mzilikazi's headquarters grew.

The first effort in the direction of a mission to Mzilikazi's people was taken by the Paris Evangelical Missionary Society, with the help of Moffat. The site chosen was Mosega (near the present-day Zeerust), among the Bahurutsi people, a tribe who paid tribute to the Ndebele of Mzilikazi. During 1831 and 1832 the French missionaries began to build a mission station on the pattern of Kuruman, an irrigated garden being the object of their greatest efforts. By the end of 1832 they had begun to have a little hope of success with the Bahurutsi when some of Mzilikazi's emissaries were killed and Mzilikazi retaliated by destroying Mosega and driving the Bahurutsi to the south and west. The French gave up at Mosega,

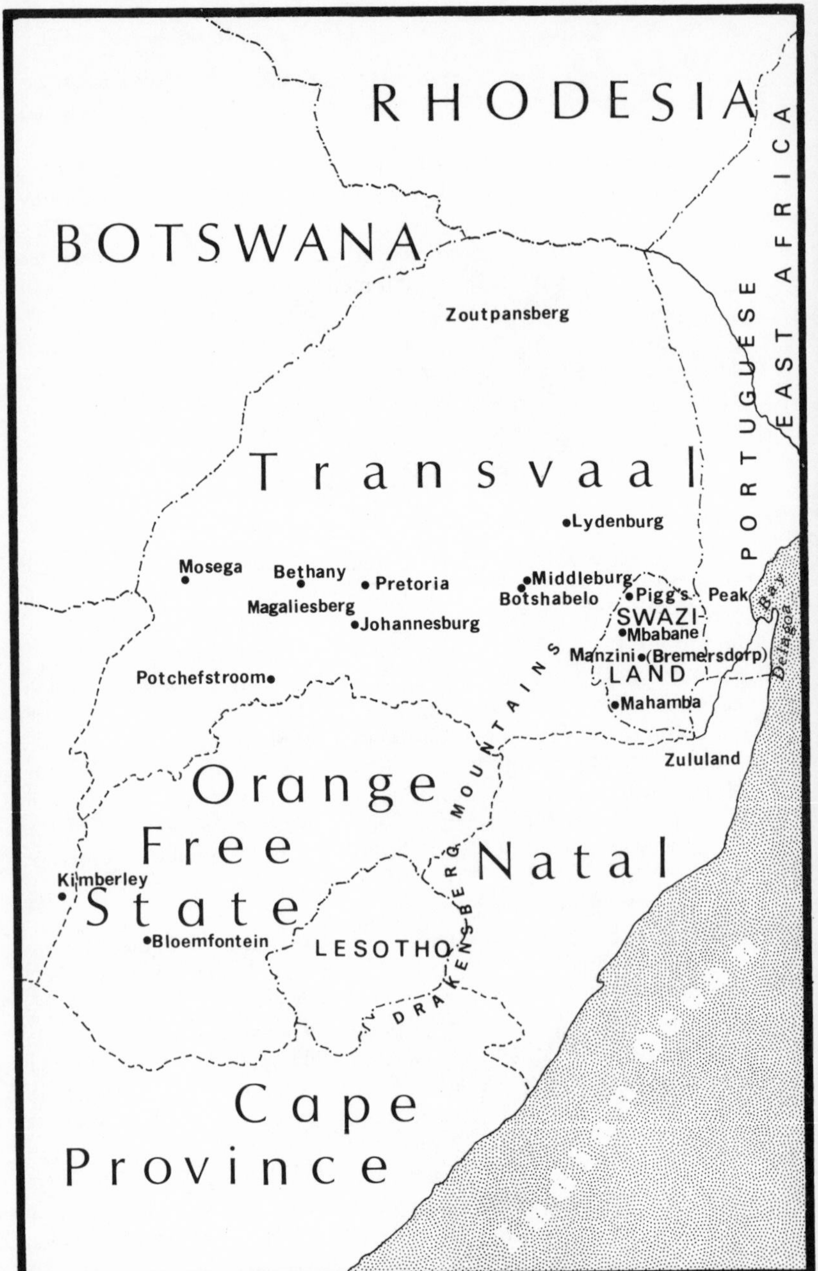
RHODESIA
BOTSWANA
PORTUGUESE EAST AFRICA
Zoutpansberg
Transvaal
Lydenburg
Mosega
Bethany
Pretoria
Magaliesberg
Johannesburg
Middleburg
Botshabelo
Pigg's Peak
SWAZI-LAND
Mbabane
Manzini (Bremersdorp)
Mahamba
Delagoa Bay
Potchefstroom
Zululand
Orange Free State
Kimberley
Bloemfontein
LESOTHO
DRAKENSBERG MOUNTAINS
Natal
Cape Province

since the people they were serving had left; some of the Bahurutsi clustered around the French missionaries at Motito, much nearer Kuruman.

Another attempt to build a mission station at Mosega took place in 1836, this time by missionaries of the American Board (Lindley, Venable and Wilson) among some of Mzilikazi's own people. They were there less than a year, however, when a Boer army attacked the place. The Ndebele people crammed into the mission house for protection and the bullets of the Boers whizzed through the windows. The American missionaries had already had a hard time, all of them having been laid up for weeks with some kind of fever, and Mrs. Wilson having died. When the Boers destroyed Mosega, the missionaries concluded that all hope of success with Mzilikazi's people was finished. Mzilikazi was, indeed, forced to move north of the Limpopo River, leaving the Transvaal open to the Boers. Whether the American missionaries might have been able to do significant mission work if they had trekked north with the Ndebele is impossible to say. Instead, they went back to Thaba Nchu with the Boers, then travelled on, by way of Grahamstown and the Transkei, to join their brethren in Natal.

The last effort at Mosega was by the Church Missionary Society. The Rev. Francis Owen, when he was forced out of Natal in 1838, looked around for another opportunity for mission work. He had heard about Mosega from Daniel Lindley, and decided that he would try there. He was accompanied by two laymen, Wallace Hewitson and Robert Philip, who arrived too late to go to Zululand. Unfortunately, the Ndebele people had fled to the north and the Bahurutsi people had not returned, so there were no people at Mosega with whom to work. After a few months, Owen packed up and returned to England.

During the 1840's and 1850's, the LMS was expanding north-wards among the Batswana. Some of their stations were in the area now incorporated in the Transvaal, but all of these were affected by the Boer expansion in the Transvaal. The Batswana were pushed farther west into the Kalahari desert and the missionaries were evicted by the Boers.

The Boers were not opposed to all missionaries, so when they evicted the LMS from the western Transvaal, they invited the Hermannsburg Mission, which had recently settled in Natal, to take their place. From 1857 to 1864 Mr. Schulenburg of the Her-

mannsburg Mission worked among the Bakwena people. During part
of the time he was alone among them, but in 1860, while he
was temporarily absent, the LMS took up work among the Bakwena
again (this was west of the Transvaal border). For some years
Schulenburg and Mackenzie cooperated together, but the Superintendent of the Hermannsburg Mission did not like this policy, so
Schulenburg was withdrawn. About the same time an opportunity
offered itself in the Magaliesberg district, west of Pretoria. Here an
African who had first heard of Christianity from the Americans at
Mosega and had later lived for some time at Thaba Nchu, where he
was baptized David Magatha, had come home to his own tribe and
preached to them. The chief became interested and wanted a
missionary to come. The Hermannsburg Mission took up the work
there. From there (Bethany) the work spread throughout the
western Transvaal.

In the eastern Transvaal a Lutheran mission was also the pioneer.
In 1860 Merensky and Grützner of the Berlin Mission tried to start a
mission among the Swazi people. They were no more successful than
Allison had been seventeen years before. Since they could not work
among the Swazis they asked permission of the Boers of the
Lydenburg Republic to settle in their area and work among the
Bapedi. The Boers agreed, but the Bapedi were not eager to have
them. For several years there were real difficulties until, in 1864, the
Berlin Mission purchased a farm, Botshabelo, where the converts
could live in peace, away from the chief and his fury. This became
the center for extension into other areas (among the Bavenda and
later among the Lovedu) and for mission institutions. Rivalry over
the chieftainship created instability and warfare among the Bapedi
for many years, and warfare between the Bapedi and the Transvaal
Republic also disturbed mission work. When Sekhukhuni, the Pedi
chief, was finally defeated by the British and imprisoned in Pretoria
(during the period of the British annexation of the Transvaal,
1877-1881), the site of his old home was granted to the Berlin Mission
Society. Previously, Merensky, the pioneer missionary, had been
appointed Representative of the Boers among the Bapedi; to what
extent this was a cause of Sekhukhuni's turning against the
missionaries soon after is difficult to ascertain. The Rev. J. A. Winter,
one of the missionaries who reestablished the mission in the Bapedi
territory after the war with Sekhukhuni was over, decided to live
according to the customs of the Bapedi. For this he was expelled from
the Berlin Mission. He founded the Pedi Lutheran Church – a

missionary-founded separatist church. The Christian Bapedi usually live in separate villages, though the Christians still observe many of the tribal customs — marriage customs, treatment by the *ngaka* (sorcerer) in time of illness, and customs having to do with new-born babies.

The Lovedu people of the northern Transvaal live in an isolated mountainous area. Their language is different from that of any of the tribes around them, and their government, presided over by a woman whose main function is to control the rain, is also quite different from that of either the Basotho or the Batswana. An anthropologist, Dr. Eileen Krige, studied the Lovedu in the 1930's (*Realm of the Rain Queen*). She found that many of the Lovedu were attending school and that, though generally rudimentary as educational establishments, these schools were helping the people adjust to modern conditions. Christians, however, were not highly regarded. There were more illegitimate births among Christian families than among pagan families. Though beer parties were frowned upon by the church, Christian men still attended them. Some of the Christians had been allied with Europeans who exploited the Lovedu. Perhaps worst of all, the Lovedu saw the church as a business proposition in which one pays for baptism, confirmation, even communion. Dr. Krige also found that many of those most influenced by the schools and the church had permanently moved from the tribal area to Pretoria or Johannesburg.

Another early mission in the Transvaal was that of the Dutch Reformed Church from the Cape. In 1957 the Synod of the Dutch Reformed Church appointed a committee to make provision for mission work outside the Cape (ironically, it was this same synod that voted to organize separate congregations for non-white Dutch Reformed Church members). There were no clergy available in South Africa to lead such a mission, though the committee was able to raise funds for the venture. Therefore missionaries were sought overseas, and found: Alexander McKidd from Scotland and Henry Gonin from Switzerland. In 1861 McKidd went to the Zoutpansberg in the northern Transvaal and Gonin went to the Bakgatla people in the western Transvaal. The result of Gonin's work, carried on for many years by himself and then by others, was the Dutch Reformed work in Botswana at Mochudi. In the Zoutpansberg, McKidd did not live long. He was succeeded by the Rev. Stephanus Hofmeyr. Hofmeyr worked there many years among the Basotho, the half-caste Buys tribe, and the

Boer farmers. From his base, DRC exploring groups went as far north as Malawi, where a mission was founded, as well as among the Shona people near Fort Victoria in Rhodesia.

The Dutch Reformed Church among the Boers of the Transvaal had a history of unpleasant disagreements during the third quarter of the nineteenth century (the early years of the South African Republic — also known as the Transvaal Republic). Most pioneer trekkers in the area were Doppers by persuasion. At that time, the British government could still exercise a certain amount of control of the Cape Synod. Furthermore, some of the clergy at the Cape were suspected of liberal ideas from their connections with Dutch universities. Therefore none of the Boers, Doppers or orthodox, wanted to be intimately connected with the Cape Synod at that time. And thus the Hervormde Kerk, the Church of the Transvaal, was organized when a clergyman from Holland arrived to serve these people. Another Dutch clergyman also arrived, whose views were quite similar to those of the Doppers, and so this segment organized a separate church — the Gereformeerde Kerk. Eventually the Cape Synod was also represented. Thus the three DRC bodies that exist now were all present in the Transvaal in the late nineteenth century. The Hervormde Kerk established its theological training in Pretoria, the Gereformeerde in Potchefstroom.

The Swiss Mission grew out of the French Mission in Lesotho. The Swiss Reformed churches had supported the Paris Society, but in the early 1870's some of the Swiss churches felt that they wanted a mission of their own. Two Swiss missionaries, Ernest Creux and Paul Berthoud, who had served for several years in Lesotho, undertook to start a new mission in the northern Transvaal among the Magwamba people (known as the Knob Noses). Three Basotho evangelists helped in the early years. After pursuing this work for some time, the missionaries discovered that the Magwamba are really the same as the Tsonga people, the bulk of whom live in Portuguese East Africa (Mozambique). The Swiss Mission extended its work across the border and became the most important mission in southern Mozambique. For a time the early Swiss missionaries had a hard time with the Transvaal government, some of them even being jailed briefly. From the northeastern part of the Transvaal, where they started their work, the Swiss Mission spread, not only eastwards into Mozambique, but also southwards through the mountainous areas of the eastern Transvaal and into Pretoria and the Johannesburg area.

Hospitals were an important part of their work at the main mission stations.

The earliest Anglican churches in the Transvaal were organized around Englishmen, a few of whom were farmers, but most of whom were miners or engaged in businesses that grew up when the mines opened. Thus the first churches were in the eastern Transvaal, where the gold rush developed around Barberton. One or two of these churches survived the collapse of the gold rush. In the early 1870's Bishop Wilkinson of Zululand visited the Transvaal. He recruited men to study for the priesthood and ordained some deacons and priests, including men who had been Methodist ministers. He laid out "circuits" of places where services should be held, and he bought property for churches and rectories. In 1874 there were three deacons and three priests in the Transvaal. The first bishop, Henry B. Bousfield, arrived in Pretoria in 1879. He had agreed to accept the bishopric only after the Transvaal had been annexed by Britain, but soon after his arrival (1881) the British withdrew when the antagonism of the Boers was forcibly expressed at the battle of Majuba. Bousfield felt that the British withdrawal was a great defeat for the Anglican Church in the Transvaal. Projects which had been started during the period of the British annexation went by default. But the discovery of gold on the Witwatersrand (Johannesburg) changed the whole picture. The greatest possible expansion did not take place in Bousfield's time because the bishop did not get along with the priest, J. T. Darragh, and the people of Johannesburg. Nevertheless work began among the white miners who came from all over the world and among the African workers, many of whom came from areas where the gospel had never been preached.

During the Anglo-Boer War, 1899-1902, the Anglican Church was inevitably identified with the English side. After the war, the Church of England sent to South Africa a group of clergymen as a Mission of Help — some prominent, some young but quite capable. These men visited every parish in the country, and took back to England a knowledge of South Africa and of what the Anglican Church was trying to do there that was very helpful in gaining support, both in men and money. In the early years of the twentieth century, the Bishop of Pretoria was W. M. Carter, who had already served as Bishop of Zululand. He was very concerned about developing the African work of the church, especially about modernising the church machinery and using the resources which were available in the cosmopolitan area Johannesburg had become. The Community of the Resurrection was invited to work among the Africans in the townships of Johannesburg, where the members not only helped to build churches and served them as priests, but also undertook social welfare work, education, and theological training. Father Huddlestone is probably the best known of the Fathers of the Community, but among the Africans of the townships all the Fathers have had the reputation of being genuine friends to those in need. In *Down Second Avenue*, Ezekiel Mphahlele pays tribute to St. Peter's School, run by the Community of the Resurrection, as a place where every boy felt loved as well as taught.

The earliest Catholic work in the Transvaal was a matter of serving scattered Catholic families, as had been the first Catholic undertakings in each area of South Africa. At first, the Transvaal was included in the territory of the Bishop of Natal; in 1866, however, Kimberley was established as the center for a new vicariate to include the Orange Free State, Griqualand West, Lesotho, and the Transvaal. The rapid growth of white communities around the mining areas provided the Catholics with opportunities to provide much needed services in education and health. Catholic orders were the first to build schools and hospitals in many towns.

Some of the Catholic orders attempted to run schools for whites and non-whites together; but, as they quickly discovered, this did not work north of the Orange River. They continued, though, to provide education for non-whites as well as whites. Orphanages and hospitals also served the non-whites. These institutions, as symbols of God's love, have often been the reason why Africans and Coloureds became Catholics. In recent years, the action of the Catholic Church in maintaining its schools after the withdrawal of government aid (after the Bantu Education Act of 1954) has led many of the intelligentsia among the non-whites to feel that the Catholic Church is the only church that really opposes the government. The fact that the altar in the Catholic Church is open to Catholics of all races contributes to this same feeling. Whereas during the first half of the nineteenth century most non-whites who were Christians belonged to nonconformist churches, in the twentieth century the Anglican and Catholic churches have had a much faster rate of growth.

The nonconformist church that has kept up the fastest growth rate is the Methodist Church. Holden, an early historian of the Methodists in South Africa, wrote in 1875:

> The Wesleyan missionaries still carry out the plan, so wisely inaugurated by the late William Shaw, of commencing the work in the towns, and making them the base of operations from whence other parts can be the better acted upon and worked. The appointments in the Trans Vaal are all to European towns; but it will soon be found that as the native work rises up in the towns, it will extend from them to different parts of the outlying districts.[1]

In the year 1875 there were Methodist missionaries at Potchefstroom, Pretoria, and Lydenburg. The work at Potchefstroom had been started not by a missionary, but by David Magatha, the same ardent Christian who had led his people in the Magaliesberg to invite a Hermannsburg missionary to preach to them. His work at Potchefstroom was not easy – he was arrested by the magistrate, flogged in the street, and banished from the Transvaal. He went to Natal, but some years later, with the help of Paul Kruger, whom he had known in his Magaliesberg days, he was able to go back to Potchefstroom and reopen the school and church he had started there. Another African, Samuel Mathabathe, who had studied under Allison at Pietermaritzburg, returned to his people in the eastern Transvaal, in Sekhukhuni's territory. The old chief objected, but when he died, Mathabathe had the chance to begin preaching and teaching. He had no connection with the Wesleyan Missionary Society and no ordained minister to administer the sacraments. The Berlin Mission tried to persuade him to join them, but he refused. Finally, on his request, Mr. Hofmeyr of the Dutch Reformed Church agreed to baptize his converts and administer communion to them with the understanding that they remained Wesleyans. And finally the Wesleyan Missionary Society caught up with Samuel and incorporated his work into their own organization.

Shaw's policy of starting in the towns and working out from there was especially effective in the Transvaal, for the town-dwelling Africans were already detribalized and most ready for membership in the church. The mining communities of the Transvaal attracted large numbers of Africans, many of them from as far away as Malawi and Zambia. Some of these returned to their homes after a time, but many stayed in the urban area and became a new proletariat. The Methodist Church, as well as other churches, offered a caring community and a meaning in life for this new African proletariat as it had done for the urban masses of the industrial towns in England a century before.

The *manyanos*, African women's groups which meet for prayer and visit the sick, arose first among the Methodists. The idea spread to other churches and now every church has a *manyano*, whether it uses that name or not, and each denomination has a distinctive uniform. The Methodist uniform − a bright red blouse, black skirt, and white hat − is one of the most impressive. The differences between *manyanos* are far fewer than the similarities. The phenomenon, taken together, represents one of the most important aspects of the new African culture that exists in South Africa. The African woman living in an urban area, often as a domestic servant, faces innumerable perils − a wandering husband, tsotsi children, high prices and meager salary, police brutality, job insecurity, and frequent burglaries and stabbings. In the *manyano* she finds sisters who support her and an opportunity for emotional release through highly emotional prayers and preaching. It helps her cope with the terrors which each coming week may hold. The *manyanos* are, perhaps, one of the strongest anti-revolutionary forces in South African society.

The Methodists of the Transvaal and Swaziland were organized separately until the 1930's; they had closer ties with the British Methodist Conference, which supplied ministers and grants for mission work. The educational center for the Transvaal African work was Kilnerton Institution, near Pretoria. Another Methodist group in the Transvaal is the American Methodist Mission, which works among Batswa mine workers from Mozambique. For some years after men from Mozambique began going to the mines to work, the American Methodists had an agreement with the American Board Mission, which had followed its Zulu members from Natal to Johannesburg. By this arrangement the Congregationalists were supposed to serve the men while they were in the Transvaal, while those who were converted while working in the mines were to be ministered to by the Methodists in Mozambique. About the time of the First World War, however, the Methodists began to feel that they needed to work in the Transvaal themselves. But to this day they have never worked among any people except those of the Mozambique tribes. Because of the tight restrictions on Protestant work in Mozambique, the Methodists have sometimes found that they were able to do more missionary work when the men were on the mines than when they were at home in Mozambique. They have a mission press which produces materials in Xitswa, for the Batswa people.

Not only the Congregationalists, but every church followed the migration of its members to the City of Gold and organized one or more of its churches there. Comity had never been a reality in South Africa; it would not have survived the gold rush if it had been. New undenominational missions, such as the South Africa General Mission and those which specialized in mine workers or railroad workers, etc., also entered the field. The diversity of the population of Johannesburg produced a diversity of churches, from Greek Orthodox through main-line Protestant to separatist groups, each with its own prophet.

# XI

# SWAZILAND

The Swazi people are closely related to the Zulus, their language being only slightly different, though there was a definite Basotho population in the area in the past — these people were conquered by their Nguni (Zulu-like) neighbors. Swaziland today is a kingdom ruled by King Sobhuza II and the members of the aristocratic Dlamini clan. Now there is something of a parliamentary democracy, but the old aristocracy and its traditions are still very powerful. This is not to say that Swaziland has not been affected by the inroads of Europeans. It has. At one time Europeans had acquired control of two-thirds of all the land in the country. Much of it has been bought back, at market prices, with savings from men working on the mines and farms, so that now only about half of the land is in the hands of Europeans. Many of these are Afrikaans-speaking farmers; others are corporations which engage in mining and large-scale agriculture (forestry, sugar, cotton, pineapples, etc.).

Along with almost all of the rest of Africa, Swaziland went through a colonial period. Like Lesotho, the king and his councillors begged the British government to take over long before it actually did. And like the Basotho, they wished for this because of the encroachments of their white neighbors, who wanted their land. At first the whites had been more or less welcomed by the king. If they brought gifts to him, especially gunpowder and the equipment to use it, they were given grants of land and concessions for practically anything that anybody ever thought to make a profit out of. But the

Swazis soon came to realize that the whites could not be assimilated as subjects of the king. Even treating them as one tribal group, with a "chief" over them (the son of Sir Theophilus Shepstone), did not stop the anarchy. The South African Republic (Transvaal) wanted to take over Swaziland in order to get that much nearer the sea. During the 1890's a joint Transvaal-British committee was supposed to administer affairs. This did not work either. After the Boers were defeated in the Anglo-Boer war, Swaziland came under direct control of the British, and a protectorate government was set up. This continued until independence in October, 1968.

Just as Swaziland was one of the last bits of Africa to receive independence in the twentieth century, it was also one of the last parts of Southern Africa to receive missionaries in the nineteenth century. Two abortive attempts were made about the middle of the century, one by the Methodists and one by the Lutherans, but no permanent mission stations were established before the 1880's. In 1844 Mr. James Allison, a Methodist catechist working in what is now the southeastern corner of the Orange Free State, received an invitation from a Swazi chief to send missionaries to him. The Rev. James Allison (who had become ordained) and Richard Giddy, plus some African teachers from other mission stations, went to Swaziland to look over the situation. They left the teachers while they reported back to the brethren in the Cape. When Allison returned to Swaziland, he found that the teachers had found a ready response; and with great encouragement these men built a mission station at Mahamba in southwestern Swaziland. By 1846 a catechism and portions of Scripture had been translated into the local language and the services and schools were eagerly attended. But the success was short-lived, since the paramount chief and the local chief began fighting. Allison and hundreds of converts fled to Natal, where they established the Indaleni mission station, near Pietermaritzburg. Many years later, one of the young men who had fled from Swaziland, Daniel Msimang, went back to reopen the work at Mahamba. He had served as a teacher and catechist in Natal and was an ordained minister before he returned in the 1880's.

In 1860, the Berlin Missionary Society sent two men to open a mission in Swaziland. After a long wait of many days to interview the paramount chief, Umswazi, they were told he was interested only in obtaining guns and powder, not in the gospel. Thus they returned to Lydenburg in the eastern Transvaal and began work there.

About the same time that the Methodists reopened their work at Mahamba, the Anglicans bought two farms, one in the Transvaal, just on the border of Swaziland, and the other near the center of the country, where they hoped to establish close contact with the royal family. The Rev. Mr. Jackson, one of the pioneers, was often called upon by Umbandzeni, the paramount, for advice in the difficult days of the concession-seekers. The early hopes of the Anglicans that the royal family might come *en masse* into their fold, were, however, disappointed. Many women of the aristocratic Dlamini clan did join the Anglicans or the Methodists, or other groups, but the men have resisted to the present time.

During the 1890's a number of smaller mission groups entered Swaziland, since it was largely unoccupied at the time and yet accessible and relatively habitable climatically. The South Africa General Mission, a nondenominational society supported by conservative Christians in South Africa, Britain, and the United States, began work in Swaziland in 1890. Its members expected to do the pioneer work themselves, but hoped that churches would then take over. The loyalty of their converts and their supporters was so deep, however, that turning the work over to others was impossible. Yet, unlike some conservative societies, they do have a reputation for cooperating with other missions. During the Anglo-Boer war Swaziland was invaded by the Boers, who burned down Bremersdorp (now Manzini), the only town of any size. Because of the disruptions of the war, the missionaries were forced to leave the area for three years, but on their return found that the African evangelists had continued the work quite successfully.

In 1892 the Seventh Day Adventists and the Scandinavian Alliance Mission also went to Swaziland. The Scandinavian Alliance Mission is now known as The Evangelical Alliance Mission (T.E.A.M.), supported by the Evangelical Free Churches in the United States. Since their beginnings, the Scandinavian Alliance Mission, the South Africa General Mission, and the Church of the Nazarene Mission have cooperated, sharing a background in the worldwide revivals of the late nineteenth century. The original group of eight missionaries sent out to Africa by the Scandinavian Alliance Mission was supposed to go to Rhodesia. But when the leader of the group, Frederick Franson, a disciple of Dwight L. Moody, made an exploratory trip to find a site for the mission, he was refused by Lobengula, chief of the Ndebele. Franson then went to

Swaziland and got permission for a mission there. But by the time they were ready to go to Swaziland, all the men of the original group had died or had abandoned the venture, leaving only four single women to undertake the work. One of these was the indomitable Malla Moe. She would have none of the ritualized life on a mission station, but spent weeks at a time living in the Swazi villages, just talking with the people, and praying for their conversion. She was the only missionary who stayed on in Swaziland during the Anglo-Boer war. For a long time the results were discouraging – the Swazis loved to talk about the gospel but not to accept it. Generally they had all they needed, and they did not see much need for being "saved." But eventually she and her colleagues did gather converts – people who had been helped in illness, boys and girls who found something more than just reading and writing when they attended school, and others. Johannes Gamede, a boy who had first come to Malla Moe in order to learn to read, became an ardent evangelist and organizer of the church after a dramatic, dream-related conversion experience.

The Church of the Nazarene opened its first mission in 1910 at Pigg's Peak. Its work has spread throughout the country and has made a very significant contribution to the educational development of the country. To the present (1969), the only nurses' training school and the only teacher training school are operated by the Church of the Nazarene. This denomination opened a Bible School for training church workers in 1921. Particularly interesting in this enterprise are the annual camp meetings, held in each of eight districts, where hundreds come together for preaching and inspiration. A tradition from the American frontier has thus been transmogrified to replace the cultural functions that the chief's assemblies and annual royal ceremonies formerly filled for those who are now in the church. The first ordinations of Africans, four, were held in 1939.

A Pentecostal group also began in 1910, in the northeast corner of the country near Portuguese East Africa. Because of their scruples against taking any medicine, they had a high mortality rate, for their site was malarial. Critics of their mission felt that their very emotional approach was especially harmful to the missionary cause, because "orgies of immorality" frequently followed such highly-charged phenomena as speaking in tongues.[1]

After failing to establish a mission in Swaziland in the 1860's, the

Berlin Mission tried again' in the 1880's, this time not sending missionaries, but helping groups of their converts from the eastern Transvaal to establish communities in Swaziland. It was a good idea, but it did not work out. The converts maintained their own Christian life, but made no impact at all on the neighborhood in which they lived. Later, in the 1920's, German missionaries visited these communities and established a station near the royal village. In the 1930's there was a Lutheran hospital in Mbabane, run by a woman doctor to whom the king entrusted his numerous wives when they were ill. In 1936 this church had about 2,000 members, according to the census figures.

The Roman Catholics were the last large mission group to enter Swaziland. The area was entrusted to the Servite order, originally Austrians, later Italians. They began work in 1912, but grew very rapidly, partly because they had the resources to build schools and churches in many different places simultaneously from the beginning. Having begun when they did, the Roman Catholics have been able to receive educational grants from the start. And since their staffs are celibate and thus their expenses are so much lower than the Protestants', whose missionary families are costly, they have been able to use funds from educational grants to expand their work much more rapidly than the Protestant societies. The general approach of the Roman Catholics to the Swazis also made for a more rapid growth of their church. Most of the Protestant missions had a rigid code of morality (for example, before Malla Moe would teach young Gamede she made him give her an expensive tobacco pipe which she broke in his presence) and a long period of initiation, whereas the catechumenate of the Catholics was usually much shorter and the confessional was considered a gradual means toward a Christian ethic. The distribution of clothing and jobs was doubtless an enticement to some — all missions did this at one time or another, but the Roman Catholics were able to do it on a much larger scale than most of the others. The Catholic ceremonial worship appealed to many Swazi and seemed to them to have power, something lacking in the less emotional Protestant services.

But not even the Roman Catholics have spread as rapidly as the separatist churches. By 1940, half of all the Swazis who claimed to be Christians were members of separatist churches. After the separatists came the Methodists, then the Seventh Day Adventists, then the Anglicans and Roman Catholics, about equal in numbers, then the Lutherans, the Dutch Reformed (almost entirely whites), the Baptists, and "others." But there were twice as many heathen as all Christians put together, including the separatists.

For a time the king was tempted to form a church of his own, and he got so far as to build half an edifice at the royal village for what was to be the "Swazi National Church." But feuding among his supporters brought the project to a halt, and the king now claims an interest in Christianity but does not give his personal loyalty to any one denomination (or conform to the marriage regulations of any). That missions played an extremely important role in providing educational (and medical) services for the country is largely by default of the British administration. For while the administration provided schools for white children, all schools for Africans were run by missions and simply subsidized by the administration (except one high school, The National School, which was run by the king and his councillors). The Anglicans provided schools for Eurafricans (Coloureds, in South African terminology). Now all schools are multiracial (at least technically), but most are still run by the churches.

Mrs. Hilda Kuper made an anthropological study of the Swazi during the 1930's and has continued her observations since then. Some of her comments on Christianity and Swazi culture are interesting:

> In Swaziland the cleavage between Christians and pagans is not as sharp as in some other parts of Africa. This is partly because of the strength of the national organization, and partly because education is not identified with religion, many Swazi aristocrats being educated and not converted, and many converts being uneducated. Pagan Swazi are fairly tolerant of the Christians, but watch them critically.[2]

One of the criticisms the non-Christians make of the Christians is that the Christians often take their disputes to the missionaries instead of to the chiefs. Also, the Christians do not follow such traditional practices as levirate marriage, which are considered essential to the well-being and solidarity of the clan. Work-parties are an important part of the traditional economy; Christians do not object to doing the work, but they have refused the traditional payment in beer. Thus they had to be organized into separate parties. The non-Christians claim that the old virtue of generous hospitality is undermined by the Christian emphasis on thrift and

the inculcation of the money economy and its virtues.[3] Mrs. Kuper
herself makes a serious charge against missions:

> Christianity in Swaziland is embodied in a number of
> churches, often antagonistic to each other as well as to "pagan
> practices". The moral unity of the human society may be
> proclaimed in theory, but is denied in action. The missionaries,
> instead of introducing greater cooperation in the nation have
> accentuated differences and bolstered European domination.[4]

# XII

# THE SEPARATIST CHURCHES

Many references have been made in the preceding chapters to separatist churches. In some sense, these churches were foreshadowed in such movements as Makanda's prophetism and the cattle killing of 1857, when elements of Christian teaching were used by tribal leaders for tribal purposes. But though there are some parallels, there are also many differences. In the 1880's there were a number of instances in which African leaders began to pull away from the missionaries because they felt that the mission church was drawing too much authority away from the chief and the tribal customs. Most of these faded away as organizations, but they had some affinity with the separatist pattern, which emerged in the next decade. The primary reason why the first churches broke away to form separate groups, in the 1890's, was that the African leaders wanted to run their own church organizations. The problem became acute on the Witwatersrand (Johannesburg) when men went there from all over the country. Many of these men were leaders in their own communities. When they got to the gold mines, they began to organize preaching and prayer meetings as they had known them at home. But then, a few steps behind, came the missionaries. The missionaries, in some cases, failed to recognize the work already underway. They failed to recognize the men of their own denomination who had been leaders in their home places. They acted as if nothing could begin until the missionaries themselves began it. This was a grave mistake and a symptom of lack of trust in

African leadership. The response of many Africans, ordained ministers among them, was to break away from their denomination and start their own. The multiplicity of denominations and missions in South Africa clearly indicates white Christians did not see breaking the unity of Christian fellowship as a grave sin.

The early phase of the separatist movement was generally referred to as "Ethiopian," because some of the leaders referred to the passage in Psalm 68 that "Ethiopia shall soon stretch out her hands unto God" as meaning that the church in Africa should be governed by Africans. Some of the Ethiopian leaders made contact with the African Methodist Episcopal Church in the United States. The A.M.E. Church, however, failed to appoint a South African as bishop and chose instead an American, causing some of the African clergy to withdraw from that church. James Dwane, one of the leaders who had approached the Americans, led a group of people into the Anglican communion in a special organization called the Order of Ethiopia. It was hoped that many separatist leaders would follow his example, but this did not happen. In fact, the A.M.E. Church has continued to be influential among educated Africans in all the provinces of South Africa, and in Lesotho and Swaziland as well.

The governments of the various parts of South Africa expressed some fear that Ethiopianism might be a political movement against the government. But their attention was soon absorbed in the events of the Anglo-Boer War. After the war, especially at the time of Bambata's Rebellion in Natal (1906), the fear of Ethiopianism recurred among government officials. Only churches which had "adequate" white supervision were granted building sites in the government locations. The government of the Colony of Natal had long correspondence and a number of interviews with the American Board Mission because it did not consider Congregational polity "adequate" supervision. Eventually the matter was dropped, and a few of the Ethiopian churches, some of the oldest, received government recognition. This meant that their ministers could become marriage officers and that they could apply for church sites in government locations. By and large, these recognized churches were most like the mission churches in their organization and general outlook.

Early in the twentieth century a new group of separatist churches began to emerge. Bishop Sundkler, who has studied the separatist churches of South Africa over a long period of time, divides them into "Ethiopian" and "Zionist" groups. The Ethiopians are those whose main interest in separating was African leadership; Ethiopian churches resemble mission churches, but have Africans running them. Zionist churches are more interested in faith healing than in church government. They generally have practices relating to traditional African practices and tend to absorb traditional ideas of sickness, health, life, and death. Most Zionist groups are small, a few dozen people following a prophet who earns his livelihood as a houseboy, messenger, or something of the sort. Sometimes the prophet has a home in a rural area, where his patients/followers live from time to time. A few Zionist leaders have collected a great following. Thousands of Africans still worship Isaiah Shembe, the Black Christ, whose headquarters were near Durban. Since his death in the 1930's, they have been led by his son. The movement owns land in various parts of Natal and Zululand. The security of knowing that one can always live at a Shembe place if one is evicted from a township or farm (such evictions are everyday nightmares to South African Africans) is a strong attraction, as well as Shembe's healing power. The annual pilgrimage to the holy mountain in January and the annual weeks of dancing in July, when Shembe's followers come from all over the country to worship together, are also a powerful pull to people who feel that the glorious past of the Zulu nation is not given a prominent place in modern South African life. Because the younger Shembe (who holds a B.A. from Fort Hare University and once taught at Adams College) is willing to cooperate with the present-day government and there is no political atmosphere in the big Shembe gatherings, these affairs go on unmolested. This is generally true of the separatist groups. Their leaders are quite willing to accept Group Areas and Separate Development, so they very seldom get into trouble with the government.

The separatist groups are so fissiparous that their number continually grows. There are thousands now. Some of the older, more established groups are interested in cooperation among themselves and, occasionally, even with mission-related churches. The African Independent Churches' Association (A.I.C.A.) cooperates with the Christian Institute to provide courses in theology for separatist ministers, a cooperative women's program, and fellowship among themselves. The hope is that such theological training will help the separatists to keep the Christian elements, rather than the syncretistic non-Christian elements, upper-most in their teaching and organization.*

At present, the old fear that Ethiopianism would lead to rebellion does not seem to have much basis.

* On separatist churches see: David B. Barrett, *Schism and Renewal: an Analysis of Six Thousand Contemporary Religious Movements* (Nairobi: Oxford University Press, 1968); V. E. W. Hayward, ed., *African Independent Church Movements*. I. M. C. Research Pamphlets No. 11 (London: Edinburgh House, 1963); G. C. Oosthuizen, *Post-Christianity in Africa* (Grand Rapids: Eerdmans, 1969); B. G. M. Sundkler, *Bantu Prophets in South Africa*, rev. ed. (London: Oxford University Press, 1961).

# XIII

# THE STATE OF THE CHURCHES

The Anglo-Boer War of 1899 to 1902, disastrous as it was in many ways, was the necessary prelude to the unification of South Africa, which was consummated in 1910. Mission work was disrupted by the war, but not seriously changed by it. Probably the church most affected by the war was the Dutch Reformed Church. In the Cape the DRC churches, like the Afrikaner people, were torn by conflicting loyalties to Afrikanerdom and the Cape government. The leadership of Afrikaner nationalism shifted to the north, to the Afrikaner republics and those who had fought for them. The traditions of the Dutch Reformed Churches in the republics became more dominantly the traditions of the Afrikaans churches than in the Cape where there was less anti-British feeling to give an edge to people's nationalistic feelings. Since the republics had been defeated in the war, the churches became an opportunity for nationalistic self-expression. There have been close ties between the ministry of the Dutch Reformed Churches and the leadership of the Nationalist Party (the party in power since 1948, what was once known as the "Re-purified Nationalist Party").

Missionary concern in the Dutch Reformed Churches has increased steadily since the time of Anglo-Boer War. Much of this concern is expressed in missionary work among the non-whites of South Africa. Each racial group is organized into a separate church. The most recently organized is the DRC Indian Church (1968), which has four congregations — two in Natal, one in the Transvaal, and one in the Cape — six white missionaries, and eight Indian evangelists. Practically all of the expenses of this Indian DRC, like its Coloured and African counterparts, are paid by the missionary committees of the white DRC. The Dutch Reformed Church also engages in foreign missions with large stations in Rhodesia and Malawi. Formerly a mission existed in Nigeria also, but political feelings in West Africa made it necessary to transfer control to the Christian Reformed Churches of the United States. The pattern of separate organizations for the various racial groups fits the government policy of separate development (apartheid) quite conveniently. DRC mission committees are very generous, but they are also paternalistic.

Whereas the Dutch Reformed Churches have increased their mission staffs during the twentieth century, most mission groups have decreased theirs. For the London Missionary Society, this movement began as early as the middle of the nineteenth century when the combination of financial stringency at home and the opening up of new areas to the north brought about a reduction in personnel in South Africa. Both of these reasons operated for other overseas mission boards also. Furthermore, by the beginning of the twentieth century, most of the mission churches had ordained African clergy and trained African teachers who could take over some of the work done by missionaries. The multi-racial churches, such as the Methodists, Anglicans, and Roman Catholics, still recruited some of their white clergy overseas, but they also recruited some from the white churches in South Africa, and the control of their organizations was definitely placed in South Africa (barring the question of to what extent a Roman Catholic bishop is controlled by the papal curia). In mission-related churches where the South African church is wholly African, the problem of control and organization was more complicated. Most mission boards (or at least their representatives on the field) did not feel that their protégés were ready for full self-government, at least not as long as they were not fully self-supporting. Therefore some kind of council in which missionaries had some or all of the control, with African leaders present also, was the usual pattern of organization. Or there might be parallel church and mission structures, each with its own defined areas of responsibility. This is still the setup in many mission-related churches.

Most of the early educational ventures of the missions were aimed at providing trained leadership for the church. Since schools and churches were invariably associated, many of the first trainees were educated not only to be teachers but to lead Sunday worship as well. Later some of these teacher-evangelists were ordained — sometimes after further training, sometimes not. General education was emphasized, rather than training men purely for the ministry, because the African communities wanted teachers and because, somewhat later, the provinces (or colonial governments) paid subsidies for teachers. Thus theological education tended to become an adjunct of teacher-training institutions. This was true even at such well-staffed schools as the Lovedale Institution and Adams College.

Because the missions ran primary schools in most of the places where they had churches, they left the matter of Christian education to the primary school teachers. But in 1954 the schools were rather suddenly taken from the missions and placed under direct government supervision. The churches were quite unprepared to undertake a program of Christian education outside the schools. A few churches have worked hard to overcome this problem, producing Sunday School materials and training Sunday School teachers, but there is still a very big gap in most African churches. In the coloured communities, the churches still "manage" most of the schools, and so the assumption that day school teachers will teach Sunday School on Sundays and that the school will indoctrinate the children in the way of the denomination that sponsors the school still persists. Doubtless the Coloured Affairs Department will eventually make this a less tenable assumption.

When Fort Hare University College was organized, several of the larger denominations contributed to the building of hostels, and these hostels served as centers for theological students from those churches. But when the government took over Fort Hare, these churches felt that it would no longer be a suitable place for their theological training, though the government kept the theological department, and this gave the impetus (along with the displacement of St. Peter's because of Group Areas and the refusal of the government to allow Adams College to continue as a private school) to the founding of the Federal Theological Seminary at Alice (next door to Fort Hare), with Anglicans, Methodists, Presbyterians and Congregationalists cooperating. The Lutherans have a theological school at Umpumulo in Natal and another at Marang in the Transvaal. The Moravians have a theological school in Port Elizabeth.

The Anglicans train men at St. Bede's College in Umtata as well as in the Federal Seminary. Roman Catholic non-white students are trained at Hamanskraal in the Transvaal. O.M.I. students go to St. Joseph's near Pietermaritzburg, but other whites are trained in Pretoria. Rhodes University is the center for most of the English-speaking white Protestant churches. For the Afrikaans-speaking churches, there are theological faculties at Stellenbosch, Pretoria, and Potchefstroom, one for each of the three churches. The University of Botswana, Lesotho, and Swaziland at Roma in Lesotho also has a theological faculty. It is evident that in their theological training the churches are willing to accept the policy of apartheid which the government desires. The churches have talked about how unchristian such separation is, but they have acceded to it in their own institutions.

There has been sufficient interdenominational cooperation to get the Federal Theological Seminary organized, but not enough to make it a united school rather than a federal one. In other aspects of church life, interdenominational cooperation in South Africa has been about equally halting. The General Missionary Conference, established in 1904, was the first effort at cooperation, and it met only every few years. In the 1930's John R. Mott visited South Africa and persuaded people that the time had come for a Christian Council. This was duly organized. At first the largest of the Dutch Reformed Churches belonged to the Council, but after 1948 it withdrew. Since then, the Christian Council (recently renamed the South African Council of Churches) has been the meeting point for English-speaking church leaders, but seldom has been much more than just a matter of talk. Its greatest drawback has been that it has little contact with the ordinary members of the churches. Local and regional councils have been sporadic affairs, though recently efforts have been directed toward strengthening them. If they are to be truly interracial and also include many lay people, there will be great difficulties. In spite of paper constitutions which enable the major English-speaking denominations to call themselves multiracial, very little real contact across racial lines takes place in any denomination, certainly not among ordinary church members.

In the latter part of the nineteenth and early part of the twentieth century, African Christians from South Africa took part in the missionary pioneering into Central Africa. Some of these African missionaries continued to work in these areas for many years, but later generations of Africans have not, generally, followed in this work. The tradition has been carried on indirectly, however, through the contributions made by exiled South African Africans in other parts of Africa.

Even in the twentieth century, new missionary groups have entered South Africa from overseas. Most of these have come from the United States. The Mormons have been successful only among white South Africans. The Jehovah's Witnesses, on the other hand, have been most successful among Africans. The Assembly of God, Full Gospel, the Churches of Christ (non-organ variety), and others have been able to work among both whites and Africans. Among Afrikaans-speaking whites, the Apostolic Faith Mission, with German connections, has been very successful, in spite of the solidarity of the DRC in most rural communities. It is not really surprising that religious movements that have met the needs of people in the United States have also seemed to meet the needs of people in South Africa. The same unsettling transition from rural to urban, agricultural to industrial environment has taken place in both. The race issue is a major problem in both countries. Other similarities can easily be enumerated.

The churches are well planted in the soil of South Africa. The crucial question now is whether they are rooted firmly enough to change their environment, or whether they will simply be changed by it. Unless they become more genuinely united, the former is not likely. But miracles are a part of the work of the Holy Spirit, and there are, in all parts of South Africa, a faithful remnant who may be the saving of the nation.

# NOTES

## CHAPTER I

[1] R.F. Kennedy, *Africana Repository*, pp. 8-9.
[2] *Ibid.*, pp. 19-20.
[3] I.D. MacCrone, *Race Attitudes in South Africa*, pp. 15-16.
[4] C.W. de Kiewiet, *A History of South Africa, Social and Economic*, p. 4.
[5] H.B. Thom, ed. *Journal of Jan Van Riebeeck*, I, p. 39.
[6] MacCrone, *op. cit.*, p. 44.
[7] H.B. Thom, ed. *op. cit.*, II, pp. 258-59.
[8] George M. Theal, *History of South Africa*, IV, p. 377.
[9] *Ibid.*
[10] *Ibid.*, pp. 377-79.
[11] Sheila Patterson, *Colour and Culture in South Africa*, p. 9.
[12] Theal, *op. cit.*, p. 95.

## CHAPTER II

[1] J. du Plessis, *A History of Christian Missions in South Africa*, p. 51.
[2] *Ibid.*, pp. 52-53.
[3] *Ibid.*
[4] *Ibid.*, pp. 53-54.
[5] Lady Anne Barnard, *South Africa a Century Ago*, pp. 168-69.
[6] J.E. Hutton, *A History of the Moravian Church*, p. 269.
[7] J.S. Marais, *The Cape Coloured People*, pp. 29-30.

8 *Transactions of the Missionary Society Containing the Rev. Mr. Kicherer's Narrative of His Mission to the Hottentots and Boschemen with a General Account of the South African Missions*, II, 1804, p. 11.

9 *Ibid.*, p. 3.

10 *Ibid.*, pp. 4-8.

11 *Ibid.*, p. 12.

12 In Richard Lovett, *History of the London Missionary Society*, I, p. 522.

13 *Kircherer's Narrative*, p. 12.

14 *Ibid.*, p. 23.

15 *Ibid.*, p. 28.

16 *Ibid.*

17 W.J. Burchell, *Travels in the Interior of South Africa*, I, pp. 252-53.

## CHAPTER III

1 George M. Theal, *History of South Africa*, V, pp. 147-48.

2 Henry Lichtenstein, *Travels in South Africa in the Years 1803, 1804, 1805, and 1806*, p. 238.

3 Quoted in P.D. Idenburg, *The Cape of Good Hope at the Turn of the Eighteenth Century*, p. 84.

4 Quoted in A.D. Martin, *Doctor Vanderkemp*, p. 189.

5 *Ibid.*, p. 190.

## CHAPTER V

1 Thomas Pringle, *Narrative of a Residence in South Africa*, p. 279.

2 Quoted in W. Bird, *State of the Cape of Good Hope in 1822*, pp. 223-25.

3 William Shaw, *The Story of My Mission in South-Eastern Africa*, p. 392.

## CHAPTER VI

1 J. J. Freeman, *A Tour in South Africa*, p. 264.

2 Quoted in Richard Lovett, *History of the London Missionary Society*, I, p. 606.

3 E.B. Sargant, *Report on Native Education*, Part III, *Education in the Protectorates*, p. 50.

4 J. Mackenzie, *Ten Years North of the Orange River*, p. 474.

5 *Ibid.*, pp. 461-65.

6 *Ibid.*, p. 77.

## CHAPTER VII

1 William E. Brown, *The Catholic Church in South Africa*, pp. 180-81.

## CHAPTER VIII

1 John Widdicombe, *Fourteen Years in the Lesotho,* pp. 81-82.

## CHAPTER X

1 W.C. Holden, *A Brief History of Methodism, and of Methodist Missions in South Africa* (London, 1877), p. 395.

## CHAPTER XI

1 C.C. Watts, *Dawn in Swaziland* (London, 1922), p. 101.

2 Hilda Kuper, *The Uniform of Colour, A Study of White-Black Relationships in Swaziland,* p. 122.

3 *Ibid.,* p. 113.

4 *Ibid.,* p. 128.

# BIBLIOGRAPHY

Agar-Hamilton, J. A. I. *Native Policy of the Voortrekkers. An Essay in the History of the Interior of South Africa, 1836 – 1858.* Cape Town: Maskew Miller, 1928.
– –. *Road to the North, South Africa, 1852 – 1886.* London: Longmans, Green, 1937.
– –. *Transvaal Jubilee.* London: SPCK, 1928.
Anderson, T. A. *The Story of Pacaltsdorp and Some Reminiscences.* Port Elizabeth: privately printed, 1957.
Arbousset, T., and F. Daumas. *Narrative of an Exploratory Tour to the North-East of the Colony of the Cape of Good Hope.* Cape Town: C. Struik, 1968 (orig. Cape Town: A. S. Robertson, 1846).
Astrup, Nils, "Mission Work in Natal and Zululand," *The East and The West,* October, 1907.
Ayliff, John, and Joseph Whiteside. *History of the Abambo Generally Known as the Fingos.* Cape Town: C. Struik, 1962 (orig. Butterworth, Transkei: "The Gazette," 1912).
Backhouse, James. *Narrative of a Visit to Mauritius and South Africa.* London: Hamilton, Adams, 1844.
Baines, Thomas. *Journal of a Residence in Africa, 1842 – 1853.* Cape Town: Van Riebeeck Society, 1961.
Barnard, Lady Anne. *South Africa a Century Ago.* London, 1908.
Baynes, A. Hamilton. *South Africa.* London: Mowbray, 1908 (Handbooks of English Church Expansion Series).
Benham, Marian. *Henry Callaway, M.D., D.D., First Bishop of Kaffraria. His Life-History and Work.* London: Macmillan, 1896.
Blaikie, William G. *The Life of David Livingstone.* London: John Murray, 1908.
Bleek, W.H.I. *The Natal Diaries of Dr. W.H.I. Bleek,* trans. O.H. Spohr. Cape Town: A.A. Balkema, 1965.
Bird, W. *State of the Cape of Good Hope in 1822.* Cape Town: C. Struik, 1966 (orig. London: John Murray, 1823).

152     THE PLANTING OF THE CHURCHES IN SOUTH AFRICA

Bokwe, John Knox. *Ntsikana, The Story of an African Convert.* Lovedale: Lovedale Press, 1914.

Botha, Colin Graham. *The French Refugees at the Cape.* Cape Town: "The Cape Times," 1919.

— —. *Social Life in the Cape Colony in the 18th Century.* Cape Town: Juta, 1926.

Boyce, William B. *Memoir of the Rev. William Shaw, Late General Superintendent of the Wesleyan Missions in South Eastern Africa, Edited by His Oldest Surviving Friend.* London: Wesleyan Conference Office, 1874.

Brady, J. E. *Trekking for Souls.* Cedara, Natal: Missionary Association of Mary Immaculate, 1952.

Brandel-Syrier, Mia. *Black Woman in Search of God.* London: Lutterworth Press, 1962.

Brodhead, Chloe A.S. *Our Free Methodist Missions in Africa to April, 1907.* Pittsburgh: Aldine Printing Co., 1908.

Brookes, Edgar. *Bishop Gray and the Nature and Mission of Anglicanism.* Cape Town: Church of the Province of South Africa, 1962.

— —. *A Century of Missions in Natal and Zululand.* Durban: Natal Missionary Conference, n.d. (ca. 1935).

— —. *Colour Problems of South Africa.* Lovedale: Lovedale Press, 1934.

— —, and Colin Webb. *A History of Natal.* Pietermaritzburg: University of Natal Press, 1965.

Brown, George. *Personal Adventure in South Africa.* London: James Blackwood, 1855.

Brown, William Eric. *The Catholic Church in South Africa From Its Origins to the Present Day.* London: Burns and Oates, 1960.

Brownlee, Charles. *Reminiscences of Kaffir Life and History and Other Papers.* Lovedale: Lovedale Press, 1896.

Brownlee, Frank. *The Transkeian Native Territories: Historical Records.* Lovedale: Lovedale Press, 1923.

Bryant, A.T. *A History of the Zulu and Neighbouring Tribes.* Cape Town: C. Struik, 1964.

— —. *Olden Times in Zululand and Natal Containing Earlier Political History of the Eastern-Nguni Clans.* London: Longmans Green, 1929.

— —. *The Zulu People As They Were Before the White Man Came.* Pietermaritzburg: Shuter and Shooter, 1949.

Bulpin, T.V. *Lost Trails of the Transvaal.* Johannesburg: Nelson, 1965.

Burchell, W.J. *Travels in the Interior of Southern Africa,* 2 vols., ed. Isaac Schapera. London: Longmans, 1953 (orig. 1822, 1824).

Burnett, B.B. *Anglicans in Natal. A History of the Diocese of Natal.* Durban: Church Wardens, St. Paul's, n.d. (ca. 1953).

Calderwood, Henry. *Caffres and Caffre Missions, With Preliminary Chapters on the Cape Colony as a Field for Emigration and the Basis of Missionary Operation.* London: James Nisbet, 1858.

Calkins, Thomas M. *Umfundisi: Missioner to Zulus.* Milwaukee: Bruce, 1959.

Callaway, Godfrey. *Pioneers in Pondoland.* Lovedale: Lovedale Press, n.d.

Campbell, John. *Travels in South Africa.* 3 volumes. London: Black and Parry, 1815 and 1822.

Carlyle, J.E. *South Africa and Its Mission Fields.* London, 1878.

Carstens, W.P. *The Social Structure of a Cape Coloured Reserve. A Study of Racial Integration and Segregation in South Africa.* Cape Town: Oxford University Press, 1966.

Casalis, E. *The Basutos; or, Twenty-Three Years in South Africa.* Cape Town: C. Struik, 1965 (orig. London: James Nisbet, 1861).

Chalmers, John A. *Tiyo Soga: A Page of South African Mission Work.* Edinburgh: Andrew Elliot, 1877.

Champion, George. *Journal of the Rev. George Champion, American Missionary in Zululand, 1835 – 1839,* ed. Alan R. Booth. Cape Town: C. Struik, 1967.

Chapman, James. *Travels in the Interior of South Africa.* London: Bell and Daldy, 1868.

Chase, John Centlivres. *The Cape of Good Hope and the Eastern Province of Algoa Bay, with Statistics of the Colony.* Cape Town: C. Struik, 1967 (orig. London: Pelham Richardson, 1843).

Cheeseman, Thomas. *The Story of William Threlfall. Missionary Martyr of Namaqualand, with Some Account of Jacob Links and Johannes Jager Who Fell with Him.* Cape Town: Methodist Publishing Office, 1910.

Christofersen, Arthur F. *Adventuring with God. The Story of the American Board Mission in South Africa,* ed. R. W. Sales. Durban: American Board Mission, 1967.

Cilliers, S. P. *The Coloureds of South Africa.* Cape Town: Banner Publishers, 1963.

Clinton, Desmond K. *The South African Melting Pot. A Vindication of Missionary Policy, 1799 – 1836.* London: Longmans Green, 1937.

Colenso, J. W. *The Colony of Natal: A Journal of Ten Weeks' Tour of Visitation.* London: Macmillan, 1855.

Cory, G. E. *The Rise of South Africa,* 5 vols. London: Longmans, 1910 – 1930.

Coxill, H. Wakelin, and Kenneth Grubb. *World Christian Handbook.* London: World Dominion Press, 1962.

Dalziel, Jack. *The History of the Presbyterian Church in South Africa.* Johannesburg, St. Columba's Presbyterian Church, n.d. (mimeographed).

Davies, Horton, and R.H.W. Shepherd. *South African Missions, 1800 – 1950. An Anthology.* London: Thomas Nelson, 1954.

de Kiewiet, C.W. *A History of South Africa, Social and Economic.* London: Oxford University Press, 1941.

de Kock, Victor. *Those in Bondage. An Account of the Life of the Slave at the Cape in the Days of the Dutch East India Company.* Cape Town: Howard Timmins, 1950.

de Mist, Augusta Uitenhage. *Diary of a Journey to the Cape of Good Hope and the Interior of Africa in 1802 and 1803,* trans. and ed. Edmund H. Burrows. Cape Town: A. A. Balkema, 1954.

Dick, Mary Cowley. *David Russell, A Sketch for a Portrait.* Durban: Knox Publishing Co., 1939.

du Plessis, I.D. *The Cape Malays.* Cape Town: 1944.

du Plessis, J. *Life of Andrew Murray.* London: Marshall, 1919.

– –. *A History of Christian Missions in South Africa.* London: Longmans, Green, 1911.

Edwards, Isobel E. *The 1820 Settlers in South Africa.* London: Longmans, 1934.

– –. *Towards Emancipation: A Study in South African Slavery.* Cardiff: Gomerian Press, 1942.

Engelbrecht, J. A. *The Korannas: An Account of Their Customs and Their History with Texts.* Cape Town: Maskew Miller, 1936.

Ferguson, George P. *CUSA. The Story of the Churches of the Congregational Union of South Africa.* Paarl: Congregational Union of South Africa, 1940.

Findlay, Joan, ed. *The Findlay Letters, 1806 – 1870.* Pretoria: Van Schaik, 1954 (on Mrs. Rebecca Schreiner).

Fleming, Francis. *Kaffraria and its Inhabitants.* London: Simpkin, Marshall & Co., 1854.

Florin, Hans. *Lutherans in South Africa.* Durban: Lutheran Publishing House, 1967.

Freeman, J. J. *A Tour in South Africa, With Notices of Natal, Mauritius, Madagascar, Ceylon, Egypt and Palestine.* London: John Snow, 1851.

Gandhi, Mohandas K. *Autobiography, or The Story of My Experiences with Truth.* Ahmedabad, Navagivan, 1927.

Gardiner, Allen F. *Narrative of a Journey to the Zoolu Country, in South Africa Undertaken in 1835.* Cape Town: C. Struik, 1966 (orig. London: William Crofts, 1836).

Garrett, A.E.F. *South African Methodism. Her Missionary Witness.* Cape Town: Methodist Publishing House, n.d. (ca. 1966).

Gerdener, G.B.A. *Recent Developments in the South African Mission Field.* London: Marshall, Morgan & Scott, 1958.

Germond, Robert C., ed. *Chronicles of Basutoland, A Running Commentary on the Events of the Years 1830 – 1902 by the French Protestant Missionaries in Southern Africa.* Morija: Morija Sesuto Book Depot, 1967.

Godlonton, R., and E. Irving. *Narrative of the Kaffir War, 1850 – 1851.* London, 1851.

Goodall, Norman. *A History of the London Missionary Society, 1895 – 1945.* London: Oxford University Press, 1954.

*Go Ye Therefore. The Missionary Work of the Dutch Reformed Church (Nederduitse Gereformeerde Kerk) of South Africa.* Cape Town: Church Information Offices, 1962.

Gray, Robert. *Journal of Two Visitations in 1848 and 1850.* London, 1851.

Grout, Lewis. *Zululand, or, Life among the Zulu-Kafirs of Natal and Zululand, South Africa.* Philadelphia: Presbyterian Publication Committee, 1864.

Groves, C. P. *The Planting of Christianity in Africa,* 4 vols. London: Lutherworth Press, 1948 – 1958.

Grubb, Kenneth, compiler. *The Christian Handbook of South Africa.* Lovedale: Christian Council of South Africa, 1938.

Halford, Samuel James. *The Griquas of Griqualand.* Cape Town: Juta, n.d.

Hammond- Tooke, W. D. *Bhaca Society. A People of the Transkeian Uplands of South Africa.* Cape Town: Oxford University Press, 1962.

Hance, Gertrude. *The Zulu Yesterday and Today. Twenty-Nine Years in South Africa.* New York: Fleming Revell, 1916.

Hayward, Victor E. W. *African Independent Church Movements.* London: Edinburgh House Press, 1963.

Hepburn, J. D. *Twenty Years in Khama's Country and Pioneering among the Batauana of Lake Ngami.* London: Hodder and Stoughton, 1896.

Hewitt, J. A. *Sketches of English Church History in South Africa, 1795 – 1848.* Cape Town: Juta, 1887.

Hewson, Leslie A. *An Introduction to South African Methodists.* Cape Town: Standard Press, 1950.

Hinchliff, Peter. *The Anglican Church in South Africa. An Account of the History and Development of the Church of the Province of South Africa.* London: Darton, Longman & Todd, 1963.

– –. *John William Colenso, Bishop of Natal.* London: Nelson, 1964.

Holden, W. C. *A Brief History of Methodism, and of Methodist Missions in South Africa.* London: Wesleyan Conference Office, 1877.

– –. *The Past, Present and Future of the Kaffir Races.* London: Richards, Glanville, 1866.

Holt, Basil. *Greatheart of the Border. A Life of John Brownlee, Founder of King William's Town.* Unpublished manuscript.

– –. *Joseph Williams and the Pioneer Mission to the South-Eastern Bantu.* Lovedale: Lovedale Press, 1954.

How, Marion Walsham. *The Mountain Bushmen of Basutoland.* Pretoria: Van Schaik, 1962.

Hunter, Monica. *Reaction to Conquest. Effects of Contact with Europeans on the Pondo of South Africa,* 2nd ed. London: International African Institute (Oxford University Press), 1961.

Huss, Bernard. *Rural Organization among the Transkeian Natives.* Umtata: United Transkeian Territories General Council, 1932.

Hutton, J. E. *A History of the Moravian Church.* London: Moravian Publication Office, 1909.

Idenburg, P. J. *The Cape of Good Hope at the Turn of the 18th Century.* Leiden: 1963.

Ive, Anthony. *The Church of England in South Africa. A Study of Its History, Principles and Status.* Cape Town: Church of England Information Office, 1966.

Jabavu, D.D.T. *The Black Problem.* Lovedale: Lovedale Press, 1921.

*Jubilee of the American Missions in Natal.* Durban: American Zulu Mission, 1885.

Kay, Stephen. *Travels and Researches in Caffraria: Describing the Character, Customs, and Moral Condition of the Tribes Inhabiting that Portion of Southern Africa.* New York: Harper, 1834.

Kennedy, R. F. *Africana Repository.* Cape Town: Juta, 1965.

Kirby, Percival, ed. *The Diary of Dr. Andrew Smith, 1834 – 1836,* 2 vols. Cape Town: Van Riebeeck Society, 1939.

Kotze, D. J. *Letters of the American Missionaries, 1835 – 1839.* Cape Town: Van Riebeeck Society, 1950.

Krige, E. J. and J. D. *The Realm of a Rain Queen. A Study of the Pattern of Lovedu Society.* London: Oxford University Press, 1943.

Krüger, Bernard. *The Pear Tree Blossoms: The Story of the Moravian Church in South Africa, 1737 – 1869.* Genadendal: Moravian Book Depot, 1966.

Kuper, Hilda. *An African Aristocracy.* London: Oxford University Press, 1947.

– –. *Indian People in Natal.* Pietermaritzburg: University of Natal Press, 1960.

– –. *The Swazi, A South African Kingdom.* New York: Rinehart and Winston, 1963.

– –. *The Uniform of Colour, A Study of White-Black Relationships in Swaziland.* Johannesburg: University of Witwatersrand Press, 1947.

Latourette, Kenneth Scott. *A History of the Expansion of Christianity,* vol. 5. London: Eyre and Spottiswoode, 1945.

Latrobe, C. I. *Journal of a Visit to South Africa in 1815 and 1816.* London: Seeley, 1818.

Lee, A. W. *Once Dark Country. Recollections and Reflections of a South African Bishop.* London: SPCK, 1949.

Lewis, Cecil, and G. E. Edwards. *Historical Records of the Church of the Province of South Africa.* London: SPCK, 1934.

Lichtenstein, Henry. *Travels in Southern Africa in the Years 1803, 1804, and 1806.* Cape Town: Van Riebeeck Society, 1928.

Livingstone, David. *Missionary Travels and Researches in South Africa.* New York: Harper, 1858.

Long, Una, ed. *The Journals of Elizabeth Lees Price, Written in Bechuanaland, Southern Africa, 1854 – 1883, with an Epilogue: 1889 and 1900.* London: Edward Arnold, 1956.

Lovett, Richard. *The History of the London Missionary Society, 1795 – 1895,* 2 vols. London: Henry Frowde, 1899.

MacCrone, I. D. *Race Attitudes in South Africa.* London: Oxford University Press, 1937.

Mackenzie, Anne, ed. *Mission Life among the Zulu-Kafirs. Memorials of Henrietta Robertson, Wife of The Reverend R. Robertson, Compiled Chiefly from Letters and Journals Written to the Late Bishop Mackenzie and His Sisters.* Cambridge: Deighton, Bell & Co., 1866.

Mackenzie, J. *Ten Years North of the Orange River. A Story of Everyday Life and Work among the South African Tribes, From 1859 to 1869.* Edinburgh: Edmonston & Douglas, 1871.

Mackenzie, W. Douglas. *John Mackenzie, South African Missionary and Statesman.* London: Hodder & Stoughton, 1902.

Macmillan, W. M. *Bantu, Boer, and Briton, The Making of the South African Native Problem.* Rev. ed., Oxford: Clarendon Press, 1963.

– –. *The Cape Colour Question, A Historical Survey.* London: Faber and Cwyer, 1927.

– –. *Complex South Africa: An Economic Footnote to History.* London: Faber and Faber, 1930.

Malan, Major C. H. *Rides in the Mission Field of South Africa, Between the Kei and the Bashee Rivers, Kaffraria. Also A Visit to the Missionary Colleges of Lovedale and Healdtown, in British Kaffraria.* London: Morgan & Scott, n.d., preface 1872.

Marais, J. S. *The Cape Coloured People, 1652 – 1937.* Johannesburg: University of Witwatersrand Press, 1962.

– –. *Maynier and the First Boer Republic*. Cape Town: Maskew Miller, 1944.

Marquard, Leo. *The Peoples and Policies of South Africa,* 3rd ed. London: Oxford University Press, 1962.

– –. *The Story of South Africa*. London: Faber and Faber, 1955.

Martin, A. D. *Doctor Vanderkemp*. London: Livingstone Press, n.d. (ca. 1931).

Martindale, C. C. *African Angelus, Episodes and Impressions*. London: Sheed and Ward, 1932.

Martin, Marie-Louise. *The Biblical Concept of Messianism and Messianism in Southern Africa*. Morija: Morija Sesuto Book Depot, 1964.

Marwick, Brian Allan. *The Swazi. An Ethnographic Account of the Natives of the Swaziland Protectorate*. London: Frank Cass, 1966.

Mayer, Philip. *Townsmen or Tribesmen*. Cape Town: Oxford University Press, 1961.

Mayson, John Scofield. *The Malays of Cape Town*. Cape Town: Africana Connoisseurs' Press, 1963 (orig. Manchester: J. Galt, 1861).

McCarter, John. *The Dutch Reformed Churches in South Africa with Notices of Other Denominations*. Edinburgh: Inglis, 1869.

Meintjies, Johannes. *Olive Schreiner, Portrait of a South African Woman*. Johannesburg: Hugh Keartland, 1965.

Meiring, Jane. *Thomas Pringle, His Life and Times*. Cape Town: A. A. Balkema, 1968.

Merriman, Nathaniel James. *The Cape Journals of Archdeacon N. J. Merriman, 1848 –1855*. Cape Town: Van Riebeeck Society, 1957.

Millin, Sarah Gertrude. *God's Stepchildren*. New York: Boni & Liveright, 1924.

– –. *King of the Bastards*. London: Heinemann, 1950.

– –. *The South Africans*. New York: Boni & Liveright, 1927.

Moffat, Robert and Mary. *Apprenticeship at Kuruman. Being the Journals and Letters of Robert and Mary Moffat, 1820 – 1828,* ed. I. Schapera. London, 1951.

Moffat, Robert. *Missionary Labours and Scenes in Southern Africa*. New York: Carter, 1843.

Moister, William. *Conversations on Wesleyan Missions*. London, 1869.

Molema, S. M. *The Bantu Past and Present. An Ethnological and Historical Study of the Native Races of South Africa*. Cape Town: C. Struik, 1963 (orig. Edinburgh: W. Green, 1920).

– –. *Chief Moroka*. Cape Town, 1951.

– –. *Montshiwa, 1815 – 1896. Barolong Chief and Patriot*. Cape Town: C. Struik, 1966.

Mönnig, H. O. *The Pedi*. Pretoria: Van Schaik, 1967.

Moore, Herbert. *The Land of Good Hope*. London: SPG, 1912.

Mphahlele, Ezekiel. *Down Second Avenue*. London: Faber and Faber, 1959.

Müller, K. *Georg Schmidt*. Herrnhut, 1923.

Muller, Helgard. *The Role of the Coloured People in the Economic Pattern of the Republic of South Africa*. Grahamstown: University Publishers, 1965.

Murray, Joyce, ed. *Young Mrs. Murray Goes to Bloemfontein, 1856 – 1860*. Cape Town: A. A. Balkema, 1954.

Nathan, Manfred. *The Huguenots in South Africa*. Johannesburg: Central News Agency, 1939.

Neumark, S. Daniel. *Economic Influences on the South African Frontier, 1652 – 1836*. Stanford: Stanford University Press, 1957.

Newton, Arthur P., and Ernest Benians. *Cambridge History of the British Empire*, vol. 8. Cambridge: Cambridge University Press, 1963.

Nilsen, Maria, and Paul Sheetz. *Malla Moe*. Chicago: Moody Press, 1956.

Northcott, Cecil. *Robert Moffat: Pioneer in Africa, 1817 – 1870*. New York: Harper, 1961.

Nunns, Theodora. *The Land of Storms and Hope. A Short History of the English Church in South Africa*. Wynberg: The Rustica Press, 1921.

Nyembezi, I. N. *Umlando ka Nzondelelo (Natal Native Home Mission)*. Cape Town: Methodist Publishing House, n.d. (ca. 1960).

O'Haire, James. *Recollections of Twelve Years' Residence, viz. from July, 1863 to June, 1875, in the Western District of the Cape of Good Hope, South Africa*. Dublin: M. H. Gill, 1877.

Omer-Cooper, J. D. *The Zulu Aftermath. A Nineteenth Century Revolution in Bantu Africa*. London: Longmans, 1966.

Otte, C., ed. *The Zulu Almanac, 1967*. Durban: Lutheran Publishing House, 1967.

Owen, Frances. *The Diary of the Rev. Frances Owen, M.A., Missionary with Dingaan in 1837-38, Together with Extracts from the Writings of the Interpreters in Zulu, Messers Hulley and Kirkman*, ed. George Cory. Cape Town: Van Riebeeck Society, 1926.

Palmer, Mabel. *The History of the Indians in Natal*. Cape Town: Oxford University Press, 1957.

Patterson, Sheila. *Colour and Culture in South Africa*. London: Routledge and Kegan Paul, 1953.

Pauw, B. A. *Religion in a Tswana Chiefdom*. London: Oxford University Press, 1960.

– –. *The Second Generation. The Study of the Family Among Urbanized Bantu in East London*. Cape Town: Oxford University Press, 1963.

Philip, John. *Researches in South Africa*. 2 volumes. London: Duncan, 1828.

Philip, Robert. *The Life, Times and Missionary Enterprises of the Rev. John Campbell*. London: John Snow, 1841.

Phillips, Ray. *The Bantu in the City*. Lovedale: Lovedale Press, 1938.

Plaatje, Sol T. *Native Life in South Africa*. London: King, 1916.

Pringle, Thomas. *Narrative of a Residence in South Africa*. Rev. ed. Cape Town: C. Struik, 1966 (orig. 1834).

*A Project for the Promotion of Education in General, as Well for the Europeans as for the Native Races of the Colony of Natal, South Africa*. Pietermaritzburg: May & Davis, 1859.

Read, James, "South Africa," *The Evanglical Magazine and Missionary Chronicle*, November, 1816.

Rees, Wyn. *Colenso Letters from Natal*. Pietermaritzburg: Shuter & Shooter, 1958.

Reuling, Eleanor S. *First Saint to the Zulus*. Boston: American Board of Commissioners for Foreign Missions, 1960.

Ricards, James D. *The Catholic Church and the Kaffir.* London: King, n.d. (ca. 1879).

Rivett, A.W.L. *Ten Years' Church Work in Natal.* London: Jarrold, 1890.

Ross, J. J. *Die Sending Te Witzieshoek, Paulus Mopeli, en Andere Sake Rakenden die Sending Aldaar.* Bloemfontein: Nasionale Pers Beperk, 1930.

Sadler, Celia, ed. *Never a Young Man. Extracts from the Letters and Journals of the Rev. William Shaw.* Cape Town: Haum, 1967.

Sargant, E. B. *Report on Native Education in South Africa, Part III. Education in the Protectorates.* London: Longmans Green, 1908.

Schapera, Isaac. *The Bantu-Speaking Tribes of South Africa, An Ethnographical Survey.* Cape Town: Maskew Miller, 1959.

– –. *The Early Cape Hottentots.* Cape Town: Van Riebeeck Society, 1933.

– –. *The Khoisan Peoples of South Africa.* London: Routledge, 1930.

– –. *Married Life in an African Tribe.* London: Faber and Faber, 1940.

– –. *Migrant Labour and Tribal Life. A Study of Conditions in the Bechuanaland Protectorate.* London: Oxford University Press, 1947.

Schimlek, Francis. *Against the Stream. Life of Father Bernard Huss, C.M.M., The Social Apostle of the Bantu.* Mariannhill: Mariannhill Press, 1949.

Schlyter, Herman. *The History of the Cooperating Lutheran Missions in Natal, 1912 – 1951.* Durban: Lutheran Publishing House, 1953.

Sedding, E. D. *Godfrey Callaway, Missionary in Kaffraria, 1892 – 1942. His Life and Writings.* London: SPCK, 1945.

Semple, D. W. *Emgwali Girls' Institution, 1861 – 1961.* Lovedale: Lovedale Press, n.d.

– –. *A Scots Missionary in the Transkei.* Lovedale: Lovedale Press, 1965.

Shaw, Barnabas. *Memorials of South Africa.* London: Mason, 1840.

Shaw, William. *The Story of My Mission in South-Eastern Africa.* London: Hamilton, Adams & Co., 1860.

– –. *Memoirs of Mrs. Anne Hodgson.* London, 1836.

Shepherd, R.H.W., ed. *Brownlee J. Ross, His Ancestry and Some Writings.* Lovedale: Lovedale Press, 1948.

– –. *Lovedale, South Africa. The Story of a Century, 1841 – 1941.* Lovedale: Lovedale Press, 1941.

Sillery, Anthony. *Bechuanaland Protectorate.* London: Oxford University Press, 1952.

– –. *Founding a Protectorate: History of Bechuanaland, 1885 – 1895.* The Hague: Mouton & Co., 1965.

– –. *Sechele, The Story of an African Chief.* Oxford: George Ronald, 1954.

Skota, T. D. Mweli, ed. *The African Yearly Register. Being an Illustrated National Biographical Dictionary (Who's Who) of Black Folks in Africa.* Johannesburg: R. L. Esson & Co., 1931.

Smith, Edwin W. *African Ideas of God. A Symposium.* London: Edinburgh House Press, 1950.

– –. *Great Lion of Bechuanaland. The Life and Times of Roger Price, Missionary.* London: Independent Press, 1957.

– –. *The Life and Times of Daniel Lindley (1801 – 1880).* New York: Library Publishers, 1952.

– –. *The Mabilles of Basutoland.* London: Hodder & Stoughton, 1939.

Smith, Thornley. *The Earnest Missionary. A Memoir of the Rev. Horatio Pearse.* London: Wesleyan Mission House, 1868.

− −. *Memoir of the Rev. John Whittle Appleyard, Wesleyan Missionary in South Africa.* London: Wesleyan Mission House, 1881.

Soga, J. H. *The AmaXosa: Life and Customs.* Lovedale: Lovedale Press, 1932.

− −. *The South-Eastern Bantu.* Johannesburg: Witwatersrand University Press, 1930.

South African Native Races Committee. *The South African Natives. Their Progress and Present Condition.* London: John Murray, 1908.

Spilhaus, M. Whiting. *The First South Africans and the Laws Which Governed Them Including the Diary of Adam Tas.* Cape Town: Juta, 1949.

− −. *South Africa in the Making, 1652 − 1806.* Cape Town: Juta, 1966.

Stavem, O. *The Norwegian Missionary Society: A Short Review of Its Work Among the Zulus.* Stavanger: Norwegian Mission Society, 1918.

Steedman, A. *Wanderings and Adventures in the Interior of Southern Africa,* 2 vols. London: Longmans, 1835.

Stevens, R. P. *Lesotho, Botswana, and Swaziland: The Former High Commission Territories.* London: Pall Mall, 1967.

Stock, Eugene. *The History of the Church Missionary Society, Its Men and Its Work.* London: Church Missionary Society, 1899.

Stow, G. *Native Races of South Africa.* London: Sonnenschein, 1905.

Sundkler, B.G.M. *Bantu Prophets in South Africa.* 2nd ed. London: International African Institute (Oxford University Press), 1961.

Taylor, James Dexter. *The American Board Mission in South Africa. A Sketch of Seventy-Five Years.* Durban: American Board Mission, 1911.

− −. *Christianity and the Natives of South Africa.* Lovedale: General Missionary Conference of South Africa, n.d. (c.a. 1927).

Theal, George McCall. *History of South Africa.* Star ed., 9 vols. Cape Town: Struik, 1964.

− −. *Willem Adriaan van der Stel and Other Historical Sketches.* Cape Town: Maskew Miller, 1913.

Thom, H. B. *The Journal of Jan Van Riebeeck,* 3 vols. Cape Town: A. A. Balkema, 1958.

Thompson, George. *Travels and Adventures in Southern Africa.* London: Colburn, 1827.

*Transactions of the Missionary Society Containing the Rev. Mr. Kicherer's Narrative of His Mission to the Hottentots and Boschemen with a General Account of the South African Missions,* no. 1, vol. 2. London: Directors of the Missionary Society, 1804.

Trollope, Anthony. *South Africa,* 2 vols. London, 1878.

Tucker, Frederick N., "On Native Education," *Natal Witness,* 24 April, 1895.

Tyler, Josiah. *Forty Years Among the Zulus.* Boston: Congregational Sunday School and Publishing Society, 1891.

*Uplifting the Zulus. Seventy-Five Years' Mission Work in Natal and Zululand.* Durban: Natal Missionary Conference, 1911.

van de Sandt, B. J., ed., *The Cape of Good Hope Almanac and Annual Register for 1847.* Cape Town: Van de Sandt, Robertson, and Collard, 1847.

van Jaarsveld, F. A. *The Awakening of Afrikaner Nationalism, 1868 – 1881.* Cape Town: Human & Rousseau, 1961.

Vilakazi, Absolom. *Zulu Transformations. A Study of the Dynamics of Social Change.* Pietermaritzburg: University of Natal Press, 1962.

Visser 't Hooft, Willem. *Christianity, Race and the South African People: Report on an Ecumenical Visit.* New York: World Council of Churches, 1952.

Walker, Eric A. *The Great Trek,* 2nd ed. London: Adam and Charles Black, 1938.

– –. *History of Southern Africa,* 3rd ed. London. Longmans, 1962.

– –. *W. P. Schreiner, A South African.* London: Oxford University Press. 1937.

Wanger, W. *Catholic Zulu Terminology. An Explanatory Supplement to the Zulu Catechism by the Same Author.* Mariannhill: Mariannhill Press, 1913.

Watts, C. C. *Dawn in Zwaziland.* London, 1922.

Wells, James. *Stewart of Lovedale. The Life of James Stewart.* London: Hodder & Stoughton, 1909.

Whiteside, J. *History of the Wesleyan Methodist Church of South Africa.* London: Elliot Stock, 1906.

Widdicombe, John. *Fourteen Years in Basutoland. A Sketch of African Mission Life.* London: The Church Printing Co., 1891 (also published as *In the Lesotho.* London: SPCK, 1895).

– –. *Memories and Musings.* London: George Allen & Unwin, 1915.

Willoughby, W. C. *Race Problems in the New Africa.* Oxford: Clarendon Press, 1923.

Wilson, Monica, and Leonard Thompson, ed. *The Oxford History of South Africa,* vol. 1, *South Africa to 1870.* Oxford: Clarendon Press, 1969.

Wright, William. *Slavery at the Cape of Good Hope.* London: Longmans, 1831.

Young, B. A. *Bechuanaland.* London: Her Majesty's Stationery Office, 1966.

# INDEX

162